THE HOLY HOUSE OF LORETO AND THE BATTLE OF LEPANTO

The Holy House of Loreto and the Battle of Lepanto

Dr. ant

Saint Norbert Media, Inc.

Contents

1

Table of Contents

The Holy House of Loreto and the Battle of Lepanto

by

Dr. ant

The Holy House of Loreto and the Battle of Lepanto

Contents

Introduction

The annals of history are etched with moments that define the rise and fall of empires, the surge of faith, and the essence of human valor. Among these, the events that intersect faith and conflict stand as critical turning points, shaping destinies of civilizations and religious beliefs alike. The saga of the Holy House of Loreto, the devout recitation of the Holy Rosary, and the epic Battle of Lepanto form a triad of such transformative occurrences. United by belief and galvanized by the fervor of Divine intervention, these narratives resound not merely in the pages of history but echo profoundly in the heart of Roman Catholic thought and European geopolitics.

In attempting to unravel the significance of these intertwined narratives, it's incumbent upon us to exercise a multi-faceted approach. The history and lore surrounding the Holy House of Loreto are saturated with both legend and documented fact, a confluence that's no less sacred to the devout than it is perplexing to historians. Consistently, we find that the edifice's terrestrial journey from Nazareth to its present sanctuary in Loreto, Italy, is cloaked in the mystery of Divine will. This journey defies the mere mechanics of relocation and touches upon the miraculous interventions attributed to Divine providence.

Equally integral to our exploration is the veneration of the Holy Rosary. When examining its origins and ascendency as a spiritual shield, the Rosary's role transcends mere piety. It's a beacon of unity and hope, rallying the faithful across continents and centuries. The Rosary becomes especially pivotal when placed within the context of the Battle of Lepanto. Pope St. Pius V's invocation of the Rosary as a powerhouse of spiritual warfare, and its adoption by the forces aligned against the Ottoman Empire, imbue the battle with an aura of sanctity.

Amidst the convergence of these elements is the Battle of Lepanto itself—an epic confrontation that was as much a clash of cultures as it was a decisive military engagement. In an era where the Ottoman Empire's expansionist agenda posed a formidable threat to Christendom, Lepanto was nothing short of a watershed. Here, not only did European naval prowess and alliance-building play critical roles, but the deep-seated faith of those involved redefined the battle as a Crusade under the auspices of Divine favor.

The significance of Lepanto isn't confined to the immediate aftermath; its repercussions were felt across centuries, altering the course of naval warfare and recalibrating the political landscape of Europe. The intricate dance of strategies, alliances, and leadership that characterized the Holy League's approach to the battle underscores a level of sophistication in military thought that reflected the broader Renaissance ideals of the time.

What then, of the pivotal figures that orchestrated and partook in these events? Among them, Pope St. Pius V stands out, not merely as a spiritual leader but as a strategist who understood the blending of temporal and spiritual realms. His ability to marshal the Christian forces and infuse them with a sense of righteous purpose adds a layer of depth to our understanding of the period. Figures such as Don Juan of Austria, and the various commanders who contributed to the Holy League's triumph, are also indispensable in recounting this chapter of history.

This book endeavors to offer a holistic view of these intertwined narratives, elucidating the sacred and the strategic, the miraculous and the tactical. Our journey will take us through the mystical passages of Loreto, across the meditative cadence of the Rosary, and into the heart of the tumultuous waters of Lepanto. By weaving together strands from various domains of knowledge—historical documentation, theological insights, and strategic analyses—we aim to present an account that resonates with the devout, the scholar, and the strategist alike.

As we traverse these intertwined stories, it becomes evident that the Holy House of Loreto, the Holy Rosary, and the Battle of Lepanto cannot be extricated from one another. They form a cohesive narrative, each element amplifying the significance of the other. The journey of the Holy House serves as a testament to the enduring faith of Christians across generations. The Holy Rosary's role as both a spiritual weapon and a unifying prayer highlights its unique position in Catholic devotion and European history. Lepanto, with its vivid depiction of conflict and resolution backed by faith, stands as a monumental episode where spirituality and military strategy converged.

Thus, the purpose of this work is to offer an in-depth exploration that does justice to the complex interplay of faith, strategy, and history. By doing so, we aspire to not only recount events but also imbue our readers with a deeper appreciation of the profound impacts these episodes have had on the world we live in today. The Holy House of Loreto, the Holy Rosary, and the Battle of Lepanto are not relics of a bygone era; they are vibrant symbols whose relevance echoes through the corridors of time, influencing contemporary faith and geopolitical paradigms.

In conclusion, our exploration will navigate through the realms of the sacred and the strategic, illuminating how these epochs of history have carved indelible marks on the fabric of Christian Europe and beyond. From the mystic translations of Marian shrines to the solemn chants of the Rosary, leading to the harrowing clashes on the Mediterranean seas, this volume encapsulates the stories that continue to inspire, guide, and empower.

Chapter 1: The Historical Context of the Battle of Lepanto

To grasp the gravity of the Battle of Lepanto, one must understand its historical context, situated in an era marked by the meteoric rise of the Ottoman Empire and the defensive posturing of the Christian European powers. The Ottoman Turks, having already seized Constantinople in 1453, sought dominion over the Mediterranean, posing a formidable threat to Christendom. The European continent, fragmented by religious and political strife, found an unlikely but necessary unity in the face of this encroachment. It was a period where the sword and the cross were inextricably linked, with both sides emboldened by deep spiritual convictions. The Ottoman naval prowess seemed invincible, their galleys roving the seas with an almost mythic ferocity, yet Christian Europe, galvanizing a coalition of maritime nations, prepared for an epic confrontation. Understanding this backdrop is vital for appreciating not just the ensuing clash, but also the fervent prayers, the strategic maneuvers, and the profound sense of destiny that would define the Battle of Lepanto, a battle not just fought on the waves, but within the very soul of a civilization.

The Rise of the Ottoman Empire

The roots of the Ottoman Empire's emergence can be traced back to the late 13th century, around 1299, when Osman I declared independence from the Seljuk Sultanate. This nascent empire, initially a small principality in northwestern Anatolia, would grow to become one of the most powerful and enduring empires in history. The early Ottomans were proficient in leveraging both military prowess and astute governance to consolidate power and expand their territory.

The empire's expansion reached a pivotal moment under the rule of Sultan Mehmed II, also known as Mehmed the Conqueror. In 1453, the Ottomans achieved a monumental victory with the conquest of Constantinople. This event signified not just the end of the Byzantine

Empire but also the ascendancy of the Ottomans as a dominant force in both Eastern Europe and the Mediterranean. Constantinople, later renamed Istanbul, was strategically vital for controlling the key trade routes between Asia and Europe. The city's fall marked the definitive shift of power to the Ottomans, cementing their role as the guardians of Islam and setting the stage for future conquests.

Following Mehmed II, successive sultans continued the empire's expansion into Europe, Asia, and Africa. Perhaps the most notable among these was Suleiman the Magnificent, who ruled from 1520 to 1566. His reign is often referred to as the "Golden Age" of the Otto-man Empire. Suleiman not only extended the empire's borders to their furthest reaches but also championed administrative reforms and cultural flourishing. His legal reforms resulted in the codification of laws that would govern the empire for centuries, illustrating the Ottomans' ability to blend martial strength with sophisticated governance.

The Ottomans employed a highly effective military system known as the devshirme, or "child levy," which involved the recruitment of Christian boys from conquered European territories. These young recruits were converted to Islam and trained as Janissaries, an elite military corps that became one of the most formidable fighting forces of the time. This system ensured a steady stream of loyal and skilled soldiers who played crucial roles in many of the empire's military campaigns.

In addition to their formidable land forces, the Ottomans developed a powerful naval presence. The Mediterranean Sea, a crucial theater for both trade and warfare, became an arena where the Ottoman fleet could project its power. The capture of key islands and coastal regions not only facilitated control over maritime routes but also enabled the Ottomans to challenge the naval supremacy of European powers. This growing naval might would be a substantial factor leading up to the Battle of Lepanto.

The Ottoman Empire's expansion into Europe was marked by several significant battles and sieges. The Battle of Kosovo in 1389 and the Battle of Varna in 1444 were decisive encounters that demonstrated the Ottomans' military capabilities and their resolve to expand westward. Each victory bolstered the empire's confidence and secured more territories, further threatening the stability and political landscape of Christian Europe.

One of the more striking features of the Ottoman governance system was its tolerance towards different religious communities. While non-Muslims were considered dhimmis, through the millet system, they were allowed to practice their religion and maintain a degree of autonomy as long as they paid the jizya tax. This multifaceted approach to governance enabled the Ottomans to manage a diverse and expansive empire effectively. Nonetheless, the underlying religious tensions and the empire's Islamic identity often put it at odds with the Christian states of Europe.

Economic factors also played a significant role in the rise and expansion of the Ottoman Empire. The control of key trade routes, including those passing through the Silk Road and various maritime corridors, provided the Ottomans with substantial economic benefits. This wealth facilitated not only military campaigns but also funded architectural and cultural projects, leaving behind a legacy of monumental structures like mosques, schools, and palaces that showcased the empire's grandeur and sophistication.

The Ottomans' focus on centralization and administrative efficiency helped stabilize newly conquered territories. A sophisticated bureaucracy, often run by capable administrators selected through meritocratic principles, ensured that provinces were efficiently governed and revenues were effectively collected. The use of detailed land registries and tax records were just some of the methods that underscored the empire's administrative acumen.

Despite its internal strengths, the Ottoman Empire was not without its challenges. Internal power struggles, succession issues, and recurring rebellions in certain provinces occasionally threatened the stability of the regime. However, the empire's strategic depth and capacity for adaptive governance frequently allowed it to absorb and overcome these internal disruptions.

The religious zeal and fervor further propelled the Ottomans in their quest for expansion. Jihad, in the sense of military struggle in the name of Islam, was a potent motivator for the empire's conquests. This ideological underpinning provided a unifying force, rallying various segments of the Ottoman society around the common cause of expanding the faith and the empire. The rhetoric of holy war often resonated deeply within the empire, fueling campaigns that reverberated across the continent.

The growing power of the Ottoman Empire garnered significant attention and concern among the European Christian states. The fall of Constantinople and subsequent advances into the Balkans and Hungary starkly illustrated the Ottoman threat. European powers, often divided by their internal conflicts and political rivalries, found themselves confronting an empire that was not only geographically expansive but also ideologically driven to challenge the Christian dominions.

The competitive spirit among European states meant that efforts to form a unified front against the Ottomans were frequently hampered by mutual distrust and competing interests. However, the shared existential threat posed by the Ottomans sometimes catalyzed temporary alliances and coalitions. These fluctuating dynamics played a crucial role in the broader historical context leading up to significant conflicts, such as the Battle of Lepanto, where a rare union in the form of the Holy League was successfully forged.

The geopolitical landscape of the late 15th and early 16th centuries was a tapestry of shifting alliances, rivalries, and power struggles. It was within this complex framework that the Ottoman Empire emerged as both an agent of change and a force of continuity. Their rise reshaped the political contours of Europe, Asia, and North Africa, drawing them into protracted interactions—both hostile and diplomatic—with the established Christian powers of the era.

As we delve deeper into the events surrounding the Battle of Lepanto, it is essential to recognize the broader historical and geopolitical context in which it occurred. The rise of the Ottoman Empire was not merely a sequence of conquests but a multifaceted phenomenon involving military strategy, administrative excellence, economic acumen, and ideological fervor. Understanding this context provides valuable insights into the motivations, strategies, and outcomes of the pivotal clash at Lepanto. As we move forward, the interplay of these factors will become increasingly evident, illuminating the profound impact of the Ottoman ascendancy on the history of Christian Europe.

The Christian European Powers

By the mid-16th century, Christian Europe found itself at a crucial juncture. The Ottoman Empire's expansion posed a significant threat to the geopolitical stability and spiritual unity of Christendom. Various European powers, often at odds with each other, were compelled to reassess their enmities and forge alliances for the greater cause of preserving their way of life and their faith.

Among these powers, the Papal States, governed by Pope Pius V, played a pivotal role. The Pope was deeply aware of the external threat posed by the Ottomans and recognized the necessity of a united Christian front. To this end, he would become the spiritual and diplomatic keystone, leveraging both his religious authority and political acumen to rally disparate nations.

Spain, ruled by King Philip II, was arguably the most powerful Christian state at the time. Philip's dominions were vast, stretching from the Iberian Peninsula to the Americas. He had significant maritime resources and a formidable navy, which would prove indispensable in the impending conflict. Spain's commitment to the Catholic Church's defense was unwavering, driven both by religious conviction and political expediency.

Venice, though a republic with a long history of maritime prowess, was driven by more pragmatic concerns. Its vast trading network across the Mediterranean was increasingly jeopardized by Ottoman naval dominance. Venetian economic interests thus closely aligned with the overarching Christian mission against the Ottomans. The Venetian navy, though expert in seafaring and galleys, required the support of its European neighbors to match the formidable might of the Ottoman fleet.

The Kingdom of Naples and the Duchy of Savoy were also significant contributors, albeit with more localized motivations and resources. Their involvement underscored the pan-European nature of the coalition, illustrating that the threat posed by the Ottomans was perceived as an existential crisis by multiple Christian states, large and small alike.

Add to this intricate tapestry the involvement of the Knights of Malta, whose historical mission against Islamic piracy and incursions provided a fighting force imbued with religious zeal and tactical experience. The knights were not just symbolic crusaders but seasoned warriors strategically important in the allied fleet.

Portugal, although less directly involved in the Battle of Lepanto, offered moral support and strategic expertise gleaned from its engagement in seafaring across the Atlantic and Indian Oceans. The Portuguese maritime strategies influenced the broader naval tactics that would be employed in Lepanto.

While the larger powers had more to offer in terms of resources, smaller states and principalities played instrumental roles, providing ships, men, and logistical support. Genoa and the Papal States were notable for their strong naval traditions and contributions. The Genoese admiral Andrea Doria was a veteran commander whose expertise would be vital in coordinating the Christian fleet.

The coalition of Christian European powers was not without its internal struggles and political maneuvering. Historical enmities and conflicting imperial ambitions had to be set aside, which required diplomatic finesse and the Pope's moral authority. The Treaty of Rome in 1571 was a masterstroke of ecclesiastical diplomacy, binding these powers into the Holy League. This formalized alliance was not merely a military coalition but also a sacred vow, underscored by religious ceremonies and mutual oaths of fidelity to the cause.

Financial support was another critical element. The Church and various monarchs poured significant resources into the effort. Despite the economic strains, the magnitude of the Ottoman threat justified the enormous expenditures. There was also a significant rallying of public sentiment through sermons and religious appeals, addressing the faithful in churches across Europe. The Battle of Lepanto was thus framed not merely as a political or military endeavor but as a holy war, or crusade, against an Islamic force that imperiled the very heart of Christendom.

As preparations for the coalition fleet advanced, so did the intricate web of espionage, counter-intelligence, and naval reconnaissance. Knowing that the Ottomans were formidable adversaries with extensive naval resources and battle-hardened commanders, Christian powers invested in better armaments, improved naval tactics, and training regimens. Though differences in command structures and military traditions posed challenges, the collective effort brought forth innovations and efficiencies that would be critical in the battle to come.

The formation of this coalition of Christian European powers, while inherently complex and fraught with potential pitfalls, demonstrated a remarkable resilience and shared sense of purpose. The unity forged at this critical historical juncture proved decisive, showing that, despite internecine conflicts and deep-seated rivalries, Europe could rally under the banner of a common faith and existential threat.

The resultant Holy League was not just a coalition of convenience but a symbol of the enduring power of faith in uniting diverse nations for a greater cause. The legacy of this alliance, culminating in the Battle of Lepanto, would echo throughout history, influencing not just the fate of Europe but also the broader narrative of Christian solidarity against overwhelming odds.

This unity of purpose and spiritual resolve, underpinned by astute political and military strategies, would lead to one of the most significant naval battles in history. The Battle of Lepanto stands as a testament to what can be achieved when disparate nations come together, setting aside their differences for the greater good. The cohesion and cooperative spirit of the Christian European powers during this period would imbue future generations with a sense of pride and reverence for the sacrifice and commitment of their forebears.

Chapter 2: The Holy House of Loreto

The Holy House of Loreto stands as a symbol of profound significance in Catholic tradition, a sanctified nexus where divinity and history intersect. Embraced by legends and borne through centuries by unwavering faith, this humble abode is believed to be the very house in which the Virgin Mary lived, where the Annunciation took place, and thus, where the Incarnation began. Whisked away from Nazareth by angelic hands—so the narrative goes—this sacred edifice found its resting place in the modest town of Loreto, Italy, in the late 13th century. Chroniclers and pilgrims alike recount centuries of miracles attributed to this blessed structure. As an enduring testament to divine intervention, the Holy House has become a focal point of Marian devotion and an emblem of spiritual resilience, inspiring countless faithful, notable among them the soldiers and strategists who would later find solace and courage in its sanctity during the pivotal Battle of Lepanto.

Origins and History

The Holy House of Loreto, a structure deeply enshrined in the hearts of Roman Catholics, holds a riveting origin story that transcends geography and time. Historians trace its beginnings to the humble home of the Virgin Mary in Nazareth, a place imbued with sanctity. According to tradition, this small house was the site of the Annunciation, where the Archangel Gabriel appeared to Mary and heralded the conception of Jesus Christ. Made from simple materials like limestone and cedar, the home's modesty stood in stark contrast to its celestial significance.

Dynamics of legend and history intertwine when discussing how the Holy House journeyed from Nazareth to its current resting place in Loreto, Italy. It is widely believed that in 1291, as the Muslim armies threatened the Holy Land, the Holy House was miraculously transported by angels to a series of locations before finally settling in Loreto. While skeptics propose that the house was physically moved by human hands and transported via ships by a noble Byzantine family, often referred to as the "Angeli," both versions of the tale bear witness to divine intervention and protection.

The move from Nazareth to Loreto didn't happen overnight, though. The house purportedly landed in several places, including Tersatto in modern-day Croatia, before making its way to Loreto. At each stage, testimonies of miraculous events and appearances of angels proliferated. These occurrences were often accompanied by healings and other supernatural phenomena, further embedding the house into the sacred landscape of Catholic belief.

Loreto itself was an insignificant hilltop village before the arrival of the Holy House. Its transformation into a bustling center of pilgrimage can be traced directly to this extraordinary event. As news spread, pilgrims and devout travelers from across Europe flocked to the site, turning Loreto into a focal point of Marian devotion. The local population adapted quickly, establishing services and facilities to accommodate the growing influx of visitors.

Over the centuries, the physical structure of the Holy House has been carefully preserved and protected. In the early 16th century, to shield it from the elements and the wear of countless pilgrimages, a grand basilica was constructed around it. This not only provided a protective layer but also served to glorify the significance of the house. The Basilica della Santa Casa remains a magnificent example of Renaissance architecture, adorned with intricate frescoes, sculptures, and chapels.

The ecclesiastical authorities have not been idle in corroborating the Holy House's authenticity. Several popes have commissioned investigations and studies to authenticate the holy relic. In the 16th century, Pope Julius II initiated one such inquiry, which involved comparing the stones of the Holy House with those found in Nazareth. The findings were astonishing; the materials matched in both composition and age, lending credence to the sacred tradition.

Beyond its material authenticity, the Holy House of Loreto has exerted profound spiritual influence. The aura of sanctity surrounding it has inspired numerous saints and theologians. Saints such as Ignatius of Loyola and Teresa of Avila found in Loreto a source of immense spiritual fortitude. Their visits to the Holy House were often turning points in their spiritual journeys, causing ripples that extended through their respective missions and works.

Furthermore, the Holy House has been a catalyst for theological reflection and Marian devotion. Its presence has inspired numerous works of art, literature, and theological treatises over the centuries. In many ways, the Holy House serves not merely as a relic, but as a living testament to the mysteries of the Incarnation and the Virgin Mary's pivotal role in the divine plan.

The historical and spiritual significance of the Holy House extends beyond Catholicism. It has also been a point of fascination for scholars of architecture, anthropology, and history. The study of its materials, design, and the logistics of its transportation has yielded substantial academic inquiry. These investigations have further illuminated the interplay between faith and reason, legend and fact.

In the broader historical context, the Holy House of Loreto symbolizes the resilience of Christian faith through turbulent times. Its miraculous relocation mirrors the migratory endurance of Christianity itself, often under duress but ever-guided by divine providence. The house thus stands not only as a spiritual sanctuary but also as a metaphor for the endurance and adaptability of the Christian faith.

Today, the Holy House continues to be a vibrant center of pilgrimage and Marian devotion. Modern pilgrims who visit the site experience a continuity of spiritual heritage, connecting with centuries of devotion and prayer. The house remains a tangible link to the early days of Christianity, a touchstone for faith in an increasingly secular world.

In conclusion, the origins and history of the Holy House of Loreto are a compelling fusion of sacred tradition, historical inquiry, and theological reflection. Whether one views its miraculous transport as a matter of divine action or human endeavor under divine guidance, the Holy House stands as a monument to the enduring power of faith. As the narrative of the Holy House continues to unfold through the centuries, it beckons each generation to explore its layers of mystery, devotion, and historical significance.

The Holy House in Loreto

The Holy House of Loreto presents an awe-inspiring enigma, drawing the devout and the curious through its storied presence and miraculous history. Nestled in a serene, picturesque landscape, Loreto is more than just a geographical location; it is an anchor for faith, tradition, and divine intercession. This sanctified structure, believed to be the very house where the Virgin Mary received the Annunciation, has been a focal point of pilgrimage, prayer, and awe for centuries.

Legend holds that angels transported the Holy House from Nazareth to its current home in Loreto. This celestial relocation, as the devout recount, was no ordinary event; it was a divine affirmation of Mary's central role in salvation history. The event was so extraordinary that it etched itself into the annals of ecclesiastical lore, inspiring reverence and devotion.

Architecturally, the Holy House is both modest and profound. The unadorned exterior belies the spiritual richness within. Inside, the sacred atmosphere envelops visitors, providing a tangible connection to the sanctity of the Virgin Mary. Pilgrims often remark on the palpable sense of peace and holiness that pervades the air, a testament to the profound spiritual significance of the structure.

Loreto's Holy House is enshrined within a basilica, an imposing architectural marvel that draws the eye heavenward. This basilica, with its intricate frescoes and soaring arches, serves not just as a housing for the Holy House but as a testament to the enduring faith of generations that have safeguarded this sacred relic. The faithful who journey to Loreto find themselves within a space where the divine and the human intersect powerfully.

The significance of the Holy House transcends its physical presence. It stands as a symbol of divine providence and the maternal intercession of Mary. For Catholics, Loreto is not merely a pilgrimage destination; it is a pivotal point of connection with the divine mysteries, a locus of grace where the faithful can seek Mary's intercession with her son, Jesus Christ. The house embodies the mystery of the Incarnation, making tangible the moment when the Word became flesh.

The history of this sacred abode includes periods of peril and protection. During times of turmoil and uncertainty, the Holy House of Loreto has served as a refuge and a bastion of the faith. Through wars, desecrations, and societal upheavals, the Holy House has persisted, a quiet yet potent beacon of divine faithfulness and maternal care. The stories of those who found solace, healing, and hope within its walls add to its sacred narrative.

Devotion to the Holy House burgeoned during the Middle Ages, with the location becoming a pilgrimage site for believers across Europe. This devout tradition has continued into the present day, with millions making the journey to Loreto each year. Pope after pope, saint after saint have mentioned the significance of Loreto in their writings and prayers, further cementing its spiritual standing in the Church.

Among the rituals and devotions associated with the Holy House, the recitation of the Litany of Loreto stands out. This litany, unique in its formulation, has been a cherished prayer for centuries, calling upon the various titles of Mary. The litany serves as a reminder of Mary's manifold roles in the life of the faith—Mother of Divine Grace, Mirror of Justice, Comforter of the Afflicted, and many more.

Historical records reveal that the Holy House played a critical role in the Holy League's formation and the ensuing Battle of Lepanto. With the enemies of Christendom massing, the faithful turned their prayers to the Virgin of Loreto, seeking her intercession for victory. The connection between Loreto and Lepanto is not merely coincidental but is perceived as an orchestrated divine strategy, a celestial strategy that turned the tide of history.

A monumental testament to Marian intercession, the story of the Holy House does not end with its transportation. Many miracles and visions have been reported in connection with Loreto, further solidifying its status as a cradle of divine intervention. Documents from various periods chronicle healings, divine warnings, and prophetic visions associated with the Holy House.

In theological scholarship, the Holy House in Loreto often serves as a point of contemplation for the mystery of Mary's role in salvation history. Theologians have delved into its significance, drawing connections to biblical typologies and Marian dogmas. The sanctuary at Loreto has evolved into a theological symbol, encapsulating the essence of the Annunciation—where human history was forever altered by Mary's "fiat" or "let it be done."

The impact of the Holy House extends beyond individual piety. It has a communal dimension, embodying the Church's collective memory and witness. The pilgrimages to Loreto often culminate in communal prayers and liturgies, fostering a sense of unity and shared faith among diverse groups of pilgrims. This communal aspect reinforces the sense of the Catholic Church as a universal family, united under the mantle of Mary.

Today, the Holy House in Loreto continues to inspire. Modern pilgrims come for various reasons—to pray, to seek healing, to find solace, or simply to connect with a profound legacy of faith. The site remains as relevant now as it was in the past, a testament to its enduring power and significance. Loreto's ability to draw people from diverse backgrounds speaks to its universal appeal and the potent symbol it represents.

In summation, the Holy House in Loreto is not just a relic; it is a living testament to the interplay between divine grace and human faithfulness. It is a sacred space where the mysteries of the Incarnation and Marian intercession are made manifest. The Holy House continues to inspire, heal, and fortify the faithful, standing as a beacon of hope and divine love in an ever-changing world. As we reflect on its history and significance, we are reminded of the unbroken thread of divine providence that weaves through the tapestry of human history, a thread that is especially vibrant in the sacred space of Loreto.

Chapter 3: Saint Pius V and His Role

As the 226th Pope of the Roman Catholic Church, Saint Pius V was a formidable force in shaping the spiritual and strategic landscape of his time. His papacy, commencing in 1566, was marked by a profound commitment to the Counter-Reformation, bolstering the integrity and discipline of the Church. Saint Pius V's role in forming the Holy League, a coalition of Christian states assembled to confront the expanding Ottoman Empire, was not only pivotal but also providential. With an unyielding sense of divine mission, he orchestrated diplomatic efforts and military campaigns that culminated in the legendary victory at the Battle of Lepanto. His fervent devotion to the Blessed Virgin Mary and the promotion of the Holy Rosary unified and inspired the Christian forces. Saint Pius V's contributions extended beyond the battlefield; his papal reforms and spiritual leadership left an indelible mark on Christian Europe, reverberating through the annals of history as a testament to the power of faith and divine intervention.

Early Life and Papacy

Giovanni Pietro Carafa was born into a prestigious family in Bosco, near the town of Alessandria, in the region of Lombardy, Italy, on January 17, 1504. His family was well-regarded and possessed significant influence and resources, placing him in a favorable position from an early age. The future Pope Pius V's upbringing was rooted in the values of piety and discipline. His parents ensured that he received a comprehensive education that emphasized both religious and secular knowledge, preparing him for the ecclesiastical career that lay ahead.

Carafa's early education entrusted him to the Dominicans, a monastic order renowned for its intellectual rigor and devout commitment to the Church. He joined the order at the age of fourteen, a decision that profoundly shaped his life. Known in religious circles as Michele Ghislieri, he immersed himself in theological studies and exhibited a particular zeal for upholding Church doctrine. His academic excellence and dedication to the faith did not go unnoticed. Consequently, the Dominican Order acknowledged his potential and rapidly advanced him through its ranks.

The formative years under the Dominicans honed Michele Ghislieri's theological acumen and scholastic rigor, traits that would later distinguish his papacy. He was ordained as a priest in 1528, and his unwavering adherence to Catholic orthodoxy earned him a reputation as a fervent defender of the faith. Notably, Ghislieri found himself amid the Protestant Reformation, a period marked by substantial religious turmoil and doctrinal disputes. His unyielding stance against heretical movements was not just a testament to his religious fervor but also a protective measure for the integrity of the Church.

Ghislieri's commitment to orthodoxy led to his appointment as an Inquisitor for the Diocese of Como, where he was tasked with identifying and addressing heretical deviations. This position was not without its challenges; navigating the complexities of ecclesiastical discipline required both skill and an unshakeable commitment to the Church's doctrine. His efforts in Como earned him recognition and eventual elevation to more prominent roles, including serving as Inquisitor for the entire Lombardy region.

In 1556, Ghislieri's steadfastness and expertise were further acknowledged when Pope Paul IV appointed him as a Cardinal. This elevation was not merely ceremonial but reflected trust in Ghislieri's ability to confront the Church's internal and external challenges. As Cardinal, Ghislieri's influence expanded, allowing him to bolster the Church's defenses against the prevailing Protestant reform. He collaborated closely with other high-ranking church officials, sharing his insights and strategies to preserve Catholic orthodoxy across Europe.

Gaining recognition for his exemplary service and unwavering faith, Ghislieri's path led him to the papacy in 1566. Taking on the name Pope Pius V, his election signaled a new era focused on stringent adherence to doctrinal purity and ecclesiastical reform. Pius V's papacy was marked by an uncompromising commitment to the Counter-Reformation, a movement aimed at revitalizing and purifying the Catholic Church in response to Protestant criticisms.

One of the defining actions of Pius V's papacy was his reform of the Roman Curia, the Church's central governing body. Recognizing the need for administrative efficiency and moral integrity, he instituted significant reforms to purge corruption and other malpractices. Pius V's policies, though sometimes perceived as harsh, were instrumental in restoring a sense of discipline and piety among the clergy and laity alike. His rigorous enforcement of the Tridentine decrees underscored his dedication to the Counter-Reformation's objectives, emphasizing both doctrinal purity and pastoral care.

Pope Pius V also pursued external alliances to strengthen Christendom's position against emerging threats, notably the Ottoman Empire. His diplomatic acumen and religious fervor culminated in the formation of the Holy League, a coalition of maritime Christian states. This alliance proved instrumental in one of the most pivotal naval battles of the 16th century, the Battle of Lepanto. Pius V's resolve and strategic vision were crucial in rallying the European powers to face the Ottoman fleet, a testament to his understanding of the broader geopolitical stakes involved.

Moreover, Pius V's pastoral care extended beyond institutional reforms and military alliances. He was fervently devoted to promoting the spiritual lives of the faithful. The pope's emphasis on the Holy Rosary exemplified this commitment; he recognized this simple yet profound devotion as a means of fostering a deeper connection with God. This promotion of the Rosary was not only a reflection of his personal devotion but also an effort to fortify the spiritual resilience of the laity amid the turbulent times.

His piety also led to notable acts of charity, particularly towards the poor and suffering. Pius V personally led initiatives to distribute alms, provide shelter for the needy, and care for the sick. These acts of mercy were consistent with his belief that true reform must be accompanied by genuine pastoral concern and the practical demonstration of Christian charity.

Pius V's legacy, while deeply rooted in his role as a papal reformer and defender of the faith, extended beyond his immediate accomplishments. His contributions to ecclesiastical reform, his steadfast opposition to doctrinal deviations, and his strategic leadership during a period of significant political and religious conflict left an indelible mark on the Church. Pius V's papacy epitomized a synthesis of devout piety, intellectual rigor, and resolute leadership, shaping the Catholic Church's trajectory for generations to come.

Thus, the path from Giovanni Pietro Carafa's early life in Lombardy to his transformative papacy as Pope Pius V was marked by a series of deliberate choices and unyielding commitments. His journey reflects an unwavering dedication to the theological principles and ecclesiastical responsibilities that defined his era, casting him as one of the pivotal figures in Catholic history. Pius V's life and papacy underscore the profound impact that resolute faith, rigorous scholarship, and strategic vision can have on the religious and temporal realms, affirming his enduring legacy within the annals of Church history.

Contributions to the Christian Alliance

Saint Pius V is a towering figure in the annals of the Christian Alliance against the Ottoman Empire. His papacy is most renowned for his fervent efforts to unite the fractious Christian European powers against a common foe. Understanding his contributions requires us to delve deeper into his strategic brilliance, spiritual fortitude, and political acumen, elements that were seamlessly interwoven to forge an alliance of unprecedented strength and unity.

First and foremost, Saint Pius V's leadership was instrumental in rallying the Christian states. He recognized early on that division among the Christian nations was a significant weakness that the Ottoman Empire could exploit. His vision extended beyond the spiritual realm, embracing political and military dimensions that were crucial for the survival of Christendom. He actively engaged monarchs, doges, and other political leaders, urging them to set aside their differences for the sake of a greater cause. His diplomatic missions were relentless; his envoys traversed Europe, carrying letters with his impassioned pleas for unity.

Perhaps one of the most significant aspects of Saint Pius V's contribution was his ability to negotiate and navigate the complex web of political rivalries. The enmity between Venice and Spain, two of the principal members of the Holy League, was particularly challenging. Yet, through sheer determination and skillful diplomacy, he managed to secure commitments from both nations. His approach was not merely to demand alliance but to offer a vision of what unity could achieve—a vision that resonated deeply with the leaders he engaged.

In his wisdom, Saint Pius V understood that a unified Christian military force required not just political and military cooperation but also spiritual conviction. He thus called for widespread prayer and fasting among the Christian populace. His emphasis on the spiritual aspect of the conflict galvanized public opinion and reinforced the justness of the cause. The invocation of the Holy Rosary became central to this spiritual mobilization; Pius V himself famously supported its dissemination, believing its recitation could invoke divine aid during the impending confrontation.

The economic backing provided by Saint Pius V and the papacy cannot be overlooked. The financial costs of assembling and sustaining the Holy League's fleet were enormous. Pius V ordered the allocation of significant papal resources to support the cause. His ability to marshal these resources was a testament not only to his administrative capabilities but also to his unwavering commitment to the crusade against the Ottomans. Generous subsidies were extended to ensure that the fleet was well-equipped and the soldiers adequately provisioned.

Furthermore, the Pope's influence extended to the technical and logistical aspects of the military preparations. In an era when rapid communication was near impossible, Saint Pius V managed to synchronize the efforts of disparate states. He understood the importance of a unified command structure and supported the appointment of Don Juan of Austria as the commander of the Holy League's fleet. By backing a single, competent leader, Pius V increased the effectiveness and coherence of the allied forces.

Saint Pius V also leveraged the power of his office to instill a sense of sacred mission among the troops. Before the fleet set sail, he bestowed blessings and transmitted papal decrees that framed the conflict in terms of a holy crusade. This instillation of moral and spiritual purpose proved vital. The soldiers fought not merely as mercenaries or conscripts but as defenders of their faith, animated by a cause that transcended mundane concerns.

The strategic foresight displayed by Saint Pius V in the formation of the Christian Alliance contributed significantly to the tactical execution during the Battle of Lepanto. His advisors included some of the finest military minds of the time, and he was instrumental in ensuring their counsel shaped the operational plans. The tactical unity achieved under his spiritual and political guidance culminated in the decisive victory at Lepanto, a triumph that remains celebrated in ecclesiastical and military history.

Beyond the immediate military and political achievements, the long-term cultural and spiritual impacts of Pius V's contributions to the Christian Alliance were profound. The victory at Lepanto was seen as a validation of his rallying cry and the power of the collective Christian resolve. It also bolstered the faith among European Christians, reinforcing the belief that divine providence favored their cause. The establishment of the Feast of Our Lady of Victory was a direct outcome of this heightened spiritual fervor, linking the triumph at Lepanto with Marian devotion.

In retrospect, the contributions of Saint Pius V to the Christian Alliance were multi-faceted and profoundly influential. His political sagacity, spiritual leadership, and unwavering commitment to the defense of Christendom carved out a legacy that extended far beyond his papacy. It was his unification of the Christian powers, both in spirit and in arms, that lay the groundwork for the monumental victory at

Lepanto, altering the course of history. His efforts serve as a testament to the power of unity and faith in overcoming seemingly insurmountable odds.

The spiritual and moral vision provided by Saint Pius V in the face of adversity remains a beacon for contemporary strategists and historians. His role in the formation and success of the Christian Alliance illustrates the enduring impact of strong, principled leadership. It is a reminder that even in the most tumultuous of times, the convergence of faith, diplomacy, and strategy can shape the destiny of nations and peoples.

Chapter 4: The Formation of the Holy League

The formation of the Holy League stands as a testament to a pivotal moment in European history. When the threat of the Ottoman Empire loomed largest, Pope Pius V took decisive action, calling upon the Christian nations to unite against a common enemy. Key figures rose to this challenge, forging an alliance that transcended borders and centuries-old rivalries. Spain, Venice, and the Papal States, among others, responded to this call to arms with a shared fervor, realizing the existential stakes involved. This coalition was not merely a political maneuver but a deeply spiritual endeavor, rooted in a collective desire to defend Christendom. The Holy League's creation marked a significant confluence of faith and strategy, illuminating the profound impact of religious conviction on military alliances. As fleets gathered under the banner of the Cross, the stage was set for a confrontation that would resonate through history, showcasing the unparalleled power of unity in the face of overwhelming odds.

The Call to Arms

The Formation of the Holy League was not an event of mere convenience or political necessity; it was a divine summons to defend the

Christian faith against an encroaching menace. Amidst rising Ottoman power and European disunity, the call to arms resounded not just in the halls of power but in every chapel and monastery, reverberating through the hearts of the faithful.

In the mid-16th century, the Ottoman Empire was an indomitable force, conquering vast swathes of territory and threatening the very existence of Christian Europe. The fall of Constantinople in 1453 had already sent shockwaves throughout the continent. Islamic forces were now at the gates of Vienna, and the Mediterranean was their dominion. This stark reality demanded a response.

The answer came from a higher authority. Pope Pius V, a man of unwavering conviction, recognized the dire necessity of a united Christian front. He viewed the struggle not merely as a military confrontation but as a cosmic battle between good and evil. To him, and to every faithful Catholic, this was an existential fight for the very soul of Christendom.

Pope Pius V's call to arms was an appeal to all Christian rulers to set aside their differences and unite against the common enemy. This was no easy task, given the deeply entrenched rivalries and political animosities between European powers. Yet, the Pope's vision and diplomatic finesse managed to forge an unlikely alliance, the Holy League.

This unprecedented coalition included the Papal States, Spain, and the Venetian Republic, among others. Each member brought something invaluable to the table — Spain's formidable navy, Venice's maritime expertise, and the Papal States' spiritual leadership. The Pope's diplomatic overtures were relentless, but they had one aim: to protect Christendom.

Diverse in their languages and customs but unified in faith and purpose, these states signed the Treaty of Rome in May 1571, formalizing their alliance. The treaty was more than a political document; it was a sacred pledge, a covenant under God to defend the faith at any cost.

The rallies and proclamations in churches and public squares imbued the Christian populace with a passionate zeal. Priests and monks preached fervently about the sanctity of their mission, invoking the intercession of saints and the protection of the Blessed Virgin Mary. The Rosary became a spiritual weapon, its beads a lifeline of hope and divine intervention.

The logistical challenge of assembling a fleet was formidable. Ships had to be constructed, crews gathered, and supplies amassed. Despite innumerable hurdles, each man, from the lowliest sailor to the highest-ranking admiral, felt a profound sense of destiny. The message from the pulpits was clear: every oar stroke, every cannon shot was an act of devotion, a defense of the faith.

Saint Pius V, cannonized subsequently for his relentless dedication, became the spiritual backbone of the Holy League. He understood the importance of this moment and leveraged every ounce of ecclesiastical and temporal power at his disposal to ensure the coalition's readiness. His fervent prayers and saintly life were a source of inspiration for all involved.

In towns and villages across Europe, the faithful gathered around images of the Virgin Mary and representation of saints, imploring divine assistance. Confraternities and lay organizations called holy vigils, encouraging the populace to arm themselves spiritually for what was to come. Young and old alike took to bended knee, bridging the divide between mortal concerns and heavenly aspirations.

Financial support was equally crucial. Wealthy nobles and common folk alike contributed to the war effort, sacrificing personal luxuries for the sake of their shared Christian identity. Coffers overflowed with donations, and entire communities pooled their resources. All sectors of society were united in this cause: the preservation of their faith and way of life.

The fleet that set sail under the banner of the Holy League was not just an assemblage of ships; it was the embodiment of a sacred mission. The sailors and soldiers were imbued with a sense of divine purpose, their spirits bolstered by the knowledge that they fought not for themselves but for the glory of God and the protection of their brethren.

As the Holy League's fleet set forth from various ports, there was an undercurrent of both trepidation and exhilaration. It was a perilous journey ahead, and everyone knew the risks were enormous, but the potential rewards were immeasurable. The commanders, seasoned veterans like Don Juan of Austria, understood that their leadership was now imbued with divine expectation.

Men knelt upon the decks of their vessels, praying the Rosary, seeking the guidance and intercession of the Blessed Virgin Mary. The spiritual readiness of the fleet was deemed as crucial as its military preparedness. Holy Masses were celebrated, confessions heard, and the sacraments administered with a sense of urgency and solemnity not often seen.

The approaching clash was not merely anticipated as a military showdown but as a moment of existential decision for Christendom. Failure was not an option, as it would have led to devastating consequences for Europe. The anticipation of the divine favor was palpable, and the morale among the ranks was remarkably high.

Thus, against this backdrop of anticipatory prayers and meticulous preparations, the Holy League embarked on its historic voyage. They sailed not just as warriors but as crusaders in the truest sense, understanding that their battle was part of a grand cosmic narrative. Every prayer uttered, every oath sworn, every sail hoisted was inextricably linked to their divine mission.

The importance of this sacred endeavor reverberated through every echelon of society. Monks in secluded monasteries, nuns in cloistered convents, kings in their splendid palaces, and peasants in their humble cottages all shared a common hope and a common prayer. Their combined spiritual and material efforts fortified the Holy League as they neared the impending confrontation.

On October 7, 1571, in the waters off Lepanto, the animating spirit of the Holy League confronted the mighty host of the Ottoman Empire. It was not just a clash of fleets but a titanic struggle between two civilizations, two ways of life, and two faiths. The ships that carried the hopes of Christendom into battle were more than mere wooden constructs. They were vessels of divine will, piloted by a congregation of the devout and the courageous.

The Call to Arms had summoned a coalition like none other, bonded together by common threats and higher purposes. This unity was their greatest strength, and their faith was their guiding star. Thus concluded the prelude to an epic saga of faith, valor, and divine providence that would unfold on the waters of Lepanto.

Key Figures in the Alliance

The Holy League's formation was a monumental undertaking that brought together some of the most influential and capable leaders of the time. The alliance was a coalition of Catholic maritime states arranged by Pope Saint Pius V to oppose the Empire of the Ottoman Turks. To appreciate the scope and significance of this union, it's vital to understand the key figures who spearheaded this holy endeavor.

Pope Saint Pius V was the spiritual and strategic mastermind behind the Holy League. Ascending to the papacy in 1566, he took it upon himself to address the growing threat of Ottoman expansion into Christian Europe. Pius V was not only a spiritual leader but a shrewd diplomat and strategist. His commitment to the cause was unwavering, and he understood the necessity of unifying the often divided Christian states. His exhortations to Catholic monarchs, coupled with diplomacy and resilience, were instrumental in forming this sacred coalition.

Don Juan of Austria, the half-brother of King Philip II of Spain, emerged as the military commander of the Holy League's fleet. Though he was only in his mid-20s at the time, Don Juan's charisma and leadership were pivotal. He had a reputation as a valiant and skilled commander, one who could inspire his men even in the direst of circumstances. His appointment was a testament to the trust that the Christian monarchs placed in his abilities to lead such a critical campaign. Under his command, the fleet not only fought with valor but also showcased an exemplary level of coordination.

King Philip II of Spain, though not directly involved in the battle, was a linchpin in providing the necessary resources and political backing. Spain was a preeminent maritime power during this period, and its contribution in terms of ships, men, and finances was crucial. Philip II's involvement underscored the Spanish commitment to halting Ottoman advances. His support for Don Juan of Austria, combined with his willingness to put substantial resources toward the cause, demonstrated the significance he attributed to the Holy League's mission.

Venetian Doge Alvise I Mocenigo was another central figure. Venice, with its vast maritime empire and seasoned navy, was a crucial member of the Holy League. Under Mocenigo's leadership, the Venetian Republic committed a significant portion of its fleet to the initiative. The Doge's foresight and commitment were critical in galvanizing Venetian support, an effort marked by both political maneuvering and genuine concern for Christian Europe's fate. Venice, with its historical rivalry with the Ottomans, found in the Holy League a pivotal alliance to secure its interests and safeguard its territories.

Marcantonio Colonna, a prominent Roman nobleman and experienced admiral, played a vital role in the fleet's operations. As a representative of the Papal States, Colonna's naval expertise and leadership were indispensable. His fleet, well-drilled and fiercely loyal, was a testament to his capability as a commander. Marcantonio Colonna brought with him not only ships and men but also a tradition of Roman military excellence that bolstered the Holy League's fighting spirit.

Giovanni Andrea Doria, a Genoese admiral and descendant of the famous Andrea Doria, contributed significantly to the alliance's naval strength. The Genoese fleet, renowned for its skilled sailors and formidable warships, was a critical addition. Doria's experience and tactical acumen were invaluable in the planning and execution phases of the campaign. His leadership helped to forge a more cohesive and effective fighting force, blending the various fleets into a unified entity capable of taking on the Ottoman navy.

Habsburg Archduke Charles II of Austria also lent his support to the Holy League. While his role was more administrative and supportive than direct, his involvement was nonetheless essential. The Habsburg territories were strategically positioned and economically significant, providing logistical and financial support that sustained the League's operations. The collaboration between these territories and the broader coalition highlighted the widespread recognition of the Ottoman threat and the collective resolve to counter it.

Stephan Bathory, the voivode of Transylvania and future king of Poland, brought a unique perspective and resources to the alliance. Although his involvement was peripheral compared to the main naval powers, his commitment to the Holy League enhanced its legitimacy. Bathory's participation symbolized a broader Christian unity against the Ottoman threat, extending the League's influence beyond the central Mediterranean. His strategic insights and the potential of rallying Eastern European support were significant, even if indirectly influencing the battle's dynamics.

The role of various other nobles, military commanders, and sailors cannot be understated. Figures like Admiral Agostino Barbarigo of Venice, who valiantly fought and died in the battle, showcased immense courage and determination. Such individuals collectively embodied the fighting spirit and religious fervor that defined the Holy League. The vision and commitment of these leaders, combined with their diverse capabilities, created a potent force that would culminate in the historic victory at the Battle of Lepanto.

The unified efforts of these key figures, despite their varied backgrounds and interests, underscored a remarkable moment of Christian solidarity. The Holy League was not merely a military alliance but a testament to shared faith and purpose. The collaboration and dedication demonstrated by these leaders ensured that their collective resolve transcended individual ambitions and political differences.

It is through understanding these key figures that one can truly appreciate the complexity and magnitude of the Holy League's formation. Their individual contributions and collective efforts were instrumental in shaping the course of history, standing as a resilient bulwark against the Ottoman expansion and safeguarding Christian Europe.

The legacy of these leaders continues to be remembered not just for the victory they achieved but for the unity and resolve they inspired. The Holy League remains a testament to what can be accomplished when disparate forces come together for a common cause, driven by faith and the pursuit of a sacred mission.

Chapter 5: The Strategy Behind the Battle

In planning the Battle of Lepanto, the commanders of the Holy League understood that a balance between conventional naval tactics and innovative approaches was essential. They meticulously analyzed the strengths and weaknesses of the Ottoman fleet, positioning their galleys in a crescent formation to maximize maneuverability and defensive capability. Recognizing the strategic significance of Lepanto's narrow gulf, the Christian forces aimed to trap the Ottoman fleet, reducing its advantage in numbers and firepower. Intelligence, gathered through clandestine efforts, provided crucial insights that enabled the coordination of various contingents from Spain, Venice, and the Papal States. The deployment of the galleasses in the vanguard, serving as floating fortresses bristling with artillery, was a stroke of genius intended to disrupt and scatter the advancing Ottoman ships. This multifaceted strategy, steeped in both divine providence and military precision, set the stage for one of the most pivotal naval engagements in history, underscoring the necessity of meticulous planning and the role of faith in martial triumphs.

Naval Tactics of the Time

As the Christian and Ottoman fleets approached the waters of Lepanto, the stage was set for a monumental clash that would shape the future of maritime strategy. Understanding the naval tactics of the time provides not only a glimpse into the military ingenuity but also the sheer will of the commanders who orchestrated these maneuvers. During the 16th century, naval warfare was a complex interplay of strategy, technology, and human valor.

Naval formations were crucial. The most prevalent formation used by the Christian fleet, under the command of Don Juan of Austria, was the crescent or half-moon. This allowed the fleet to maximize the broadside capabilities of their galleys, which were armed with cannons primarily on their sides. By arranging ships in a sweeping curve, they aimed to envelop and crush the Ottoman forces from three sides. Opposing them, the Ottomans also adopted their variations of crescent formations, allowing flexibility and the ability to close gaps quickly in their line of battle.

Galleys were the dominant vessels in this era. These oared ships were ideal for the relatively enclosed and calm waters of the Mediterranean. Their ability to maneuver during close-quarter skirmishes made them indispensable. Each galley had a combination of sailors, soldiers, and oarsmen, often sitting in cruelly harsh conditions. The roles aboard were distinct: sailors managed the sails and rigging, soldiers were ready for boarding actions, and oarsmen provided the necessary propulsion for maneuvering the vessel during combat.

The key to successful naval tactics was also in the weaponry. Cannons were pivotal, and their effective use could decide the outcome of engagements. Christian forces capitalized on their advanced gunnery techniques, honing their skills to fire simultaneously—what could be described as a synchronized barrage. This concentrated firepower aimed to cripple enemy ships swiftly. The Ottomans, for their part, favored lighter, faster ships and relied on rapid enhancements to close the distance effectively, resorting often to boarding actions where their warriors excelled.

One can't overlook the ingenious designs and diverse roles of auxiliary vessels. Smaller ships, known as fustas or galliots, played supporting roles in larger battles. These nimbler boats performed reconnaissance, relayed messages, and executed flanking maneuvers, crucial for outmaneuvering larger enemy ships or breaking their lines. Additionally, bombarding vessels equipped with mortars could lob explosive shells over greater distances, causing disarray and softening the enemy before fully engaging.

A significant component of naval combat strategy was the art of ramming. The prow of the galley, reinforced with metal, was designed to cause maximum damage upon impact. The goal was to disable the opponent's ship by breaching its hull, leading to chaos and vulnerability to further attacks. Effective ramming required precise control of the vessel and precise timing to minimize the attacker's own vulnerabilities.

The winds and weather played non-negotiable roles, frequently dictating engagement strategies. Commanders had to possess an acute understanding of the natural elements. Favorable winds could turn the tide—pun intended—of battle in a moment's notice. Skilled tacticians timed their advances with the changing weather patterns, exploiting the wind to gain speed for maneuvers or to dictate the pace of engagement. A sudden storm could scatter fleets, rendering intricate plans useless and pushing naval commanders into frenetic improvisation.

In naval warfare, morale was both a weapon and a shield. A fleet with high morale would fight with relentless tenacity, while a demoralized crew could spell disaster. Clergy and chaplains played roles in boosting the spirits of the Christian fleet, invoking divine favor and fortitude, which was particularly resonant considering the religious context of the conflict. The Ottomans, too, held firm beliefs in their divine destiny, driving their warriors to feats of courage and, sometimes, acts of desperation.

Communication during battles was a sophisticated ballet. Signal flags, lanterns, and sound signals orchestrated by drums or trumpets conveyed orders across vast stretches of sea. Miscommunication could lead to disastrous mistakes; hence, captains were reliant on a predetermined set of signals that conveyed complex commands succinctly. These signaling systems had to be understood universally within a fleet, demanding rigorous training and consistency.

Strategic deception was not uncommon. Feints, false retreats, and sudden raids were tactics used to mislead the enemy. For instance, a ship feigning retreat might lure the opponent into a vulnerable position where a hidden contingent awaited to ambush. These strategic ploys required meticulous coordination and immense trust among the fleet's commanders.

The human element in these tactics cannot be underestimated. Leadership was key. Aboard each vessel, the chain of command had to act decisively as often the heat of battle left no room for hesitation. Don Juan of Austria's leadership, marked by his valor and tactical acumen, played a pivotal role in unifying and inspiring the Christian fleet. Similarly, Ali Pasha's command reflected the strength and ambition of the Ottoman forces, highlighting how personal leadership could influence the broader strategy.

The role of espionage and intelligence gathering before and during the battle was indispensable. Scouts and informants provided crucial information about enemy movements, fleet compositions, and potential weaknesses. This flow of intelligence allowed commanders to make informed decisions, adapt their strategies dynamically, and anticipate enemy maneuvers.

Additionally, logistics formed the backbone of any successful naval campaign. Securing supplies, ensuring the health and readiness of the crew, and maintaining the ships' combat capabilities required a well-organized supply chain. Armies, both on sea and land, could be rendered impotent without proper logistics, leading to lost battles even before the first cannonball was fired.

Ultimately, the naval tactics of this period were a rich blend of age-old traditions and emergent innovations. By leveraging a combination of technology, human skill, and divine faith, both the Christian and Ottoman fleets exhibited the apex of naval warfare during the 16th century. While the tactics used at Lepanto were reflective of the times, they also laid the groundwork for future maritime strategies, influencing naval warfare for centuries to come.

The Strategic Importance of Lepanto

For those studying the nuances of history, strategy, and faith, the Battle of Lepanto stands as a monumental clash that revealed the profound strategic dynamics of the Mediterranean world. The naval confrontation was not simply a battle between fleets; it was an epochal event that determined the dominance of powers in the region and underlined the strategic importance of Lepanto as a decisive location. Understanding why Lepanto was so crucial requires delving into the intricate web of geopolitical, religious, and military considerations of the 16th century.

Lepanto, located in the Gulf of Patras, was geographically and strategically significant for several reasons. Its position guarded the gateway to Western Europe, making it a bulwark against Ottoman expansion. For centuries, the Ottomans had been expanding westward, posing a significant threat to European Christendom. Control over Lepanto meant control over a critical maritime route, which was essential for trade and military movements. The stakes were not merely territorial but also spiritual, as the Ottoman Empire's advance represented a challenge to Christian Europe's religious hegemony.

Furthermore, the era's naval warfare emphasized the importance of seasoned sailors and capable ships more than ever before. The fleets that clashed at Lepanto included war galleys, a type of ship that was agile and formidable in close combat. The movement and placement of these fleets required meticulous planning and an acute understanding of naval tactics. Therefore, the location of Lepanto was not merely a happenstance battlefield but a chosen arena that maximized the strategic capabilities of the Holy League's naval forces under Don Juan of Austria and minimized the movement efficacy of the Ottoman fleet.

Additionally, the battle was underscored by a clash of civilizations, heightening the strategic importance of the location. The Ottoman Empire, under the command of Ali Pasha, sought not just to expand territorially but also to project its power across Europe. Control of the seas would mean enhanced capability to launch further incursions into European lands. Conversely, the Holy League, a coalition of European Catholic maritime states brought together by Pope Pius V, viewed Lepanto as the frontline in a broader defense of their shared Christian heritage.

The geography of the battle site itself contributed to the strategic considerations. Nestled within the Gulf of Patras, Lepanto's waters constrained the vast Ottoman fleet's mobility, providing a tactical advantage to the more nimble Holy League galleys. The narrow straits and the limited naval theater meant that tactical decisions during the battle carried enormous weight. The encirclement strategies often employed in larger sea spaces were less feasible here, leading to direct confrontations that required not just numerical strength but also superior maneuvering and coordination.

Economically, control over Lepanto would also affect the wider Mediterranean trade routes. During this period, the Mediterranean Sea was the lifeline for most European and Middle Eastern economies. Merchant vessels traversed these waters laden with goods from various parts of the world. Dominance here meant not only military supremacy but also the ability to disrupt or secure trade, which in turn would fund future military endeavors. Consequently, Lepanto wasn't just a strategic naval theater; it was an economic fulcrum for the powers engaged in the battle.

One cannot ignore the religious undertones that charged the strategic importance of Lepanto. For the Catholic states, the battle was a form of a crusade, blessed by the Holy See and imbued with a sense of divine mission. The victory at Lepanto was seen not just as a military success but as a sign of divine favor. This perception was crucial in rallying and maintaining the morale and support of various European powers. The victory was celebrated with fervor, and the Holy Rosary was credited with playing a vital role in achieving divine intercession. This aspect added layers of spiritual and psychological importance to controlling Lepanto.

All these factors combined to make the Battle of Lepanto not just a significant military engagement but a pivotal moment with far-reaching implications. The coalition forces, composed of ships from Venice, Spain, and the Papal States among others, orchestrated their strategy with an acute awareness of what was at stake. Their victory at Lepanto did not just halt Ottoman advancement into Europe but also reshaped the power dynamics in the Mediterranean. The battle's outcome emphasized the strategic importance of collective defense and highlighted the intricacies involved in naval warfare at the time.

Preserving control over Lepanto meant that European powers could bolster their defenses and ensure the sanctity and safety of Western Christendom. The victory validated the strategic foresight of the Holy League's leaders and justified the extensive efforts put into forming the alliance. Beyond the military victory, the battle of Lepanto became a symbol of Christian unity and determination, transforming it into an enduring legacy that influenced European geopolitical strategies for years to come.

In the end, the strategic importance of Lepanto can be appreciated by examining its impact on military tactics, economic control, and ideological warfare. It was a confluence of necessity and opportunity, where the timely and well-executed strategies of the Holy League thwarted the ambitions of a rising powerhouse. The site of Lepanto, both as a geographical location and as a historical milestone, remains a testament to the complex and multifaceted nature of strategic warfare during that era.

Chapter 6: The Prelude to Battle

The gathering of the fleets marked the beginning of an unprecedented endeavor. Ships from Venice, Spain, and the Papal States convened with a sense of divine purpose, bound together by the Holy League to confront the formidable Ottoman fleet. As they embarked on their journey towards Lepanto, the air was thick with both anticipation and trepidation. Sailors and soldiers alike carried with them the hopes of Christian Europe, each prayer and each glance towards the serene Mediterranean horizon a testament to their resolve. The blend of seasoned warriors and fresh recruits created a dynamic that was both fervent and somber, aware that they were part of a momentous clash of civilizations. This prelude to battle was not merely a gathering of forces; it was the assembly of a collective faith, the preparation of souls for a conflict that would resonate through history, forever entwining the sacred with the martial. Their journey wasn't just a physical progression but a pilgrimage of sorts, enshrined with the weight of their mission and the blessings of the Holy Rosary, a spiritual armor as essential as any weapon forged from steel.

The Gathering of Fleets

The confluence of naval forces from the fragmented Christian states of Europe marked a defining moment in 1571. The seas shimmered with potential as fleets began to assemble for a pivotal clash that would alter the course of history. The preparations weren't mere exercises in logistics and strategy; they carried profound spiritual and political weight, uniting disparate kingdoms under a singular, divine banner.

The odyssey began in earnest with Papal directives cascading from Rome, urging maritime powers to commit their vessels and men to a singular mission: the defense of Christendom from the advancing Ottoman threat. Pope Pius V, a pope well-versed in the gravitas of divine intervention, ardently believed that unity among Christian realms was essential. His call to arms resonated across the continent, striking a chord deep within the monarchs' hearts and minds.

Keenly aware of the stakes, Venice, still reeling from prior Ottoman incursions, responded with unparalleled zeal. The Venetian Arsenal, renowned for its efficiency and vast output, began producing galleys at an unprecedented rate. This time, the serenissima city saw not just an opportunity for revenge against their eastern adversaries but also a moral imperative to protect their faith and way of life. Genoese and Spanish fleets, veterans of Mediterranean skirmishes, likewise answered the call with formidable seafaring prowess and tactical acumen.

Into this intricate web of alliances stepped Don Juan of Austria, an illustrious figure chosen to lead the Christian armada. His calm demeanor and charismatic leadership proved instrumental in forging an uneasy yet resolute coalition. Don Juan's name became synonymous with dedication and a deep-rooted conviction that Divine Providence was guiding their endeavor.

As the fleets converged at Messina, a palpable sense of urgency and anticipation filled the air. The sailors, warriors, and officers, hailing from diverse corners of Christendom, shared stories of faith and resolved animosities in the shadow of a common adversary. Despite language barriers and varied customs, an unspoken understanding and unity emerged, reinforced daily by the recitation of the Holy Rosary—a practice encouraged by Pope Pius V himself. This act of devotion symbolized their reliance on the intercession of the Blessed Virgin Mary, whose guidance they fervently sought in the forthcoming conflict.

The strategic mind behind much of the fleet's assembly lay with Giovanni Andrea Doria, a shrewd tactician who meticulously planned the routes and safe harbors for the gathering ships. Ensuring the logistical coherence of such an expanse of naval power was no small feat. Supplies, medical provisions, and weaponry had to be stockpiled with precision, and the morale of the fighting men required constant bolstering through sermons and holy rites.

The imposing sight of the armada—an ironclad testament to the power of faith and determination—struck fear and admiration alike. Hulking galleasses, bristling with cannons, flanked the more nimble galleys, forming a disciplined yet fearsome line of battle. As ships set sail from the rendezvous point, local fishermen and townsfolk cast their eyes upon this formidable display, whispering prayers for victory and safe return.

Prayer wasn't merely a personal refuge; it served as a communal binding force. In the face of daunting odds, the words of the Psalmist offered solace. Chaplains on board provided spiritual guidance, ensuring that every soul, from the highest-ranking officers to the humblest deckhands, felt that God's hand steered their course. The chant of the "Ave Maria" harmonized with the creaks and groans of the wooden hulls, echoing across the waves as if Divine Providence itself navigated their path.

In the weeks leading to the ensign's unfurling of battle standards, covert operations and reconnaissance missions became more frequent. Espionage and intelligence gathering were crucial in anticipating

Ottoman maneuvers. Christian spies embedded within Ottoman ports relayed vital information about enemy fleet compositions and their movements, ensuring that the allied commanders could strategize effectively. These clandestine efforts highlighted the ongoing warfare that predated the open conflict, a silent prelude woven into the fabric of naval skirmishes and blockades.

The fleet not only bonded over mutual religious fervor but also through the necessity of shared survival. Practicing maneuvers, understanding the strengths and weaknesses of their vessels, and preparing contingencies for potential emergencies became the routine. It was in these exercises that the leadership of veterans like Agostino Barbarigo and Marcantonio Colonna shined, sharing their wealth of naval combat experience with less seasoned sailors.

By the crescendo of their preparations, every soul aboard had been made keenly aware of both their significance and their mortality. The banners of Christendom flew high, adorned with the image of the Virgin Mary and the crucifix, symbols that inspired courage and conviction. They saw themselves not merely as soldiers or seamen but crusaders entrusted with a divine mission. Each action, each maneuver, was laden with a sense of higher purpose that transcended the individual and united them as a force of providence.

Thus, as the gathered fleets set their course toward Lepanto, the balance of the world's future seemed to teeter in the lapping waves beneath their ships. This wasn't a mere assembly of naval power; it was a confluence of faith, strategy, and the indomitable human spirit. The Christian fleet, a marvel tethered to divine prayer and human ingenuity, sailed to confront an existential threat with hearts brimming with hope, courage, and unwavering faith in God's ultimate plan. An epic contest awaited, one that would resonate through the ages and define the realms of Christendom for generations to come.

The Journey to Lepanto

The journey to Lepanto was not merely a physical undertaking but an odyssey defined by faith, strategy, and an unwavering commitment to safeguard Christendom. As the fleets converged, worlds apart in their origins, their mission became unified by a cause greater than any single domain or power—defending the soul of Christian Europe.

As summer gave way to fall in 1571, the Mediterranean became the stage for a colossal drama. The Christian armada, a diverse coalition gathered under the banner of the Holy League, navigated through both tumultuous waters and geopolitical intricacies. Venice, Spain, the Papal States, and other contributors offered not only ships but also their finest sailors and soldiers. Their paths, leading from ports such as Naples, Genoa, and Venice, converged with urgency and anticipation.

Among them, the flagship of Don Juan of Austria, commanding admiral of the Holy League, symbolized the unity and strength of this gathered force. Don Juan, with his natural charisma and military acumen, emerged as a rallying figure. His leadership was reinforced by a deep commitment to the divine mission entrusted to him by Saint Pius V. The Pope, ever the spiritual general in Rome, implored the faithful to pray the Rosary in anticipation of the impending clash.

One cannot underestimate the tactical challenges faced by this fleet. Each captain dealt with his own set of logistical nightmares—whether replenishing supplies under threat of attack or establishing lines of communication across the sprawling waters. The armada's route was carefully charted, hugging coasts where necessary to avoid Ottoman patrols, sailing out into open seas where possible, all while maintaining a semblance of formation crucial for both defense and offense.

Morale aboard the ships varied. The veterans of countless maritime skirmishes lent their experience and tactical knowledge, knowing all too well what lay ahead. For the younger men, the voyage was a crucible of nerves and excitement. Their spirits were bolstered by daily prayers, with chaplains present to administer sacraments, fostering a palpable sense of divine guidance.

A fervent devotion to the Holy Rosary permeated the journey. Rosary beads passed from hand to hand, sailors and soldiers alike invoking the intercession of the Blessed Virgin Mary. This shared act of worship served as a profound reminder of the providential hand they believed guided them towards their fateful encounter.

As the fleet wound its way through the Adriatic, Ionian, and subsequent seas, they were in constant readiness for battle—from the smallest maneuverable galleys to the massive galleasses bristling with firepower. Shipwrights and blacksmiths worked indefatigably to keep the vessels in prime condition. Cannons were cleaned and polished; sails mended and reinforced. Every man knew that any lapse in preparedness could spell disaster.

The Ottoman forces, too, were not idle. Led by Ali Pasha, they roamed these ancient shipping lanes with both confidence and menace. They had long dominated the eastern Mediterranean, and now their eyes were set on extending their control westwards. To the eyes of the Turks, the Christian fleet, though formidable, was but another challenge in their expansive campaign to spread the influence of the Sublime Porte.

Despite scattered intelligence and occasional skirmishes, the precise location of the enemy remained an anxious uncertainty for both sides. Scouts were sent ahead, some never returning, others bringing hastily scribbled reports of sightings and potential enemy movements. These tidbits of information formed a mosaic of possibilities, stitched together by the commanders who constantly recalibrated their plans.

As they approached Lepanto, the significance of their mission resonated ever more profoundly. Lepanto, situated in the Gulf of Patras, was more than a strategic point; it was a symbolic bastion that both sides sought to control. For the Ottomans, it represented a gateway to the western Mediterranean and, subsequently, to the heart of Europe. For the Christian forces, it was a line in the sand—a declaration that the tide of Ottoman expansion must be stopped.

The final days leading to the battle were marked by a solemn yet resolute atmosphere. The sight of the opposing fleet on the horizon sent a chill down many spines but also ignited a fiery resolve. Amidst final prayers, blessings, and tactical briefings, the men prepared for the zenith of their journey. Every ship was positioned, every cannon primed, every warrior steeled for the encounter of a lifetime.

This convergence at Lepanto was more than a chapter in history; it was the climax of a journey marked by spiritual zeal, strategic brilliance, and a desperate hope for divine intervention. Ships and men, united in their diversity of origin and singularity of purpose, looked to the dawn not merely as the start of another day, but as the moment their faith and fate would be tested against the full force of an empire.

Chapter 7: The Battle of Lepanto

The morning of October 7, 1571, dawned with an uneasy quiet over the Gulf of Patras. As the sun began to rise, it unveiled a sight that would soon become historic: the vast, imposing fleet of the Christian Holy League facing off against the formidable armada of the Ottoman Empire. The air was thick with tension and the prayers of thousands of soldiers reached up to the heavens, invoking the intercession of the Virgin Mary through the Holy Rosary. The first engagements were swift and brutal, shattering the stillness as cannons roared and swords clashed. Key turning points punctuated the battle, such as the gallant charge led by Don Juan of Austria, whose leadership rallied the Christian forces. The final clash saw the Holy League victorious, a deliverance attributed not only to brilliant strategy and valiant fighting but also to divine intervention, as many believed. This epic confrontation not only halted Ottoman expansion into Europe but also signaled a potent symbol of hope and unity for Christendom, forever enshrining the Battle of Lepanto in the annals of history.

The Morning of October 7, 1571

The dawn of October 7, 1571, brought with it a sense of foreboding and anticipation across the waters of the Gulf of Patras. The morning mist hung low, almost as if the heavens themselves were holding their breath for what was to unfold. On one side, the Holy League's fleet, comprised of various Christian forces, assembled with a solemn determination. Banners fluttered gently, and the sound of rosaries being recited drifted across the decks. It was not just a battle for territory—this was a spiritual crusade, a fight for the soul of Christendom.

Don Juan of Austria, the young and charismatic commander of the Holy League, moved among his men with an air of confidence that belied his youth. He knew the enormity of the task ahead, but he also believed in the righteousness of their cause. The fleet was a striking sight: rows of galleys lined up in formation, each bristling with soldiers and artillery. The Christian banners bore the insignias of various European powers, united in this singular mission. This coalition was unprecedented, a testament to the persuasive powers of *Pope Pius V* and the collective will of the Christian states.

As the sun began to rise, casting a golden hue over the waters, the tension among the men sharpened. The calm before the storm seemed stretched to infinity, filled with silent prayers, last-minute preparations, and the steely gazes of men ready to commit themselves to the fight. Some were inspired by the tales of saints and martyrs that had laid the groundwork for this very moment. Others were driven by a more immediate fear—the ever-encroaching might of the Ottoman Empire.

No detail was overlooked in the Holy League's preparations. Sailors ensured the galleys' oars were in top condition, while soldiers adjusted their armor and weapons one last time. Highly skilled Venetian engineers made sure that the cannons were primed and correctly positioned, ready to unleash havoc on the enemy fleet. This was no mere skirmish; every element of warfare was fine-tuned to perfection.

On the other side, **Ali Pasha**, the commanding admiral of the Ottoman fleet, was equally resolute. His ships formed an imposing crescent-shaped formation—a tactical arrangement that had brought them countless victories. The Ottoman sailors and soldiers, seasoned by numerous campaigns, were confident in their abilities. They chanted in unison, a stirring reminder of their own spiritual and military convictions.

Communication between the ships was crucial, and signal flags were raised across both fleets to convey orders. From the crow's nests, scouts scanned the horizon, watching for the first signs of the enemy fleet breaking through the mist. The anticipation was a palpable force, rippling through the ranks of men on both sides. The moment of engagement was imminently nearing, and each man felt the weight of history on his shoulders.

As the Holy League's fleet advanced, Don Juan of Austria ordered the raising of a banner depicting Christ crucified, symbolizing the sacrificial nature of their quest. It was a visual testimony to their faith and an effort to imbue the men with a sense of divine purpose. Prayers echoed from ship to ship, a spiritual fortification that was as vital as any physical armor.

The quietude of that morning belied the chaos that was about to erupt. Both sides knew that the coming hours would decide more than just the control of the Mediterranean—they would determine the future of Christian Europe versus the Ottoman Empire. The morale was high on both sides, but the stakes were even higher.

Soon, the mist began to lift, and both fleets could now fully see each other. The Ottoman crescent formation was as intimidating as legends described, a looming specter of past victories. However, the Holy League's ships held steady, their resolve undiminished. Signal flags waved, the final adjustments were made, and commanders across the deck echoed the same sentiment: Trust in God.

The sounds of drums and trumpets shattered the morning stillness, signaling the final approach. Rowers plunged their oars into the sea in unison, their strokes a physical manifestation of the collective will of Christendom. As the gap between the two fleets narrowed, artillerists readied their canons, watching for the perfect moment to unleash their deadly salvo.

The first cannon fire was deafening, a thunderous roar that marked the beginning of what would be one of the most famous naval battles in history. Smoke and fire erupted from the gundecks, and the once calm sea was quickly transformed into a churning theater of war. The Holy League's galleys surged forward with renewed vigor, an armada powered by faith and unity.

Chaos reigned supreme as both fleets collided. Swords clashed, arrows flew, and cannons boomed, turning the sea red with blood and strewn with debris. Ship against ship, man against man—the battle quickly became a furious melee. Yet amid the pandemonium, there was a distinct sense of purpose on both sides. Each fleet believed that victory was within their grasp.

Amid this chaotic tapestry of war, stories of personal bravery and sacrifice began to emerge. On the Holy League's flagship, Don Juan of Austria fought valiantly, his presence on the battlefield a source of immense inspiration for his men. Elsewhere, nameless soldiers found themselves in acts of unexpected heroism, spurred on by the unfathomable stakes of the battle.

Back on shore, those who watched from afar were filled with a mix of dread and hope. They could see the plumes of smoke rising from the stricken ships and hear the distant sounds of conflict. For them, the battle was not just an epic clash of armies but an existential struggle that would define the future. Their prayers were fervent, their faith unshakable, and their hopes bound to the gallant efforts of those fighting in their name.

Only a few hours had passed since dawn, but already the morning of October 7, 1571, had seared itself into the annals of history. As the sun climbed higher, the forces of the Holy League and the Ottoman Empire contended for supremacy, both driven by forces far greater than mere worldly ambition. In the heart of the fray, it was clear that this was not just a battle for territory, but a monumental struggle for spiritual and cultural dominance.

First Engagements

The Battle of Lepanto, fought on October 7, 1571, began in the early hours of the morning as the Holy League's fleet, under the command of Don Juan of Austria, advanced towards the Ottoman forces led by Ali Pasha. The Christian fleet, comprised of ships from the Papal States, Spain, Venice, and several other European powers, formed a crescent formation designed to envelop the enemy. This initial strategic maneuver aimed to compensate for the numerical superiority enjoyed by the Ottoman navy, which had long dominated the Mediterranean.

As the two fleets drew closer, the sea itself seemed to hold its breath. The atmosphere was charged with a heady mix of trepidation and steely resolve. Don Juan, youthful and charismatic, moved among his men, bolstering their spirits with promises of victory and the protection of God. On the Catholic galleys, sailors and soldiers clutched their rosaries, a visible testament to their faith and a plea for divine intervention.

The first volleys of cannon fire shattered the morning calm, sending splintered wood and metal flying through the air. The cacophony of battle erupted as the two naval forces collided. Initial engagements were furious and chaotic, as row upon row of galleys smashed into each other, boarding parties leaping onto enemy decks with a fervor that only could be inspired by the belief in the righteousness of their cause.

Close combat ensued, with blades clashing and warriors grappling for dominance. Among the Christian ranks, the early stages of the fight saw a fierce determination. Venetian and Spanish ships, renowned for their sturdy build and firepower, concentrated their assault on the Ottoman center, where Ali Pasha's flagship, the Sultana, bristled with both firepower and resolve.

Throughout these first engagements, the element of leadership became crucial for both sides. Don Juan's flagship, the Real, became a beacon of coordination. Signal flags and messengers darted about, ensuring that different segments of the fleet could act in concert, a harmony of steel orchestrated against the might of the Ottoman Empire.

Don Juan himself was a whirlwind of activity on the deck, directing maneuvers and urging his men forward.

Despite the overwhelming pressure, the Ottomans fought back with relentless vigor. Their own galleys were lighter and swifter, able to maneuver quickly and strike unexpectedly. These first clashes revealed the tenacity of the Ottoman sailors and Janissaries, well-trained and seasoned from years of Mediterranean dominance. The battle became a brutal test of endurance and strategy, with both sides grappling for the upper hand.

The sun climbed higher, and the waves near Lepanto turned red, reflecting the fierce combat that continued without pause. Christian galleys, driven by the muscular endurance of chained rowers, slammed into the Ottoman flanks, attempting to break their lines. Each ship represented a microcosm of the larger battle, where individual acts of valor and sacrifice played out alongside collective maneuvers of military strategy.

Saint Pius V had instructed that the fleet carry an image of Our Lady of Guadalupe and ordered the Rosary to be recited by all combatants, believing in the protective power of the Virgin Mary. This spiritual element gave the Catholic forces a sense of purpose beyond mere military victory. Shouts of "Jesus" and "Maria" echoed across the water as the Christians wielded both sword and faith against their formidable adversaries.

Gradually, the impact of early successes began to shape the course of the wider battle. Certain key ships on both sides were incapacitated, leading to gaps in the formations that could be exploited or dangerously widened. The orderliness of the initial advances had given way to a more chaotic struggle, where smaller groups fought independently, yet in support of a larger, unseen strategy orchestrated by their commanders. The air was filled with the clamor of battle: the crash of colliding ships, the roar of cannon fire, the clash of steel upon steel, and the cries of the wounded.

The sight was epic in the medieval sense—an engagement of titanic forces driven by the convictions of faith, honor, and survival. For many, the first engagements were a test not just of their martial prowess but of their spiritual resolve. Many believed they were not merely participants in a battle but actors in a larger, divine drama played out on the stage of history.

On both fleets, the chain of command ensured that reinforcements were quickly deployed where needed. The Christian right wing, led by Andrea Doria, saw heavy fighting against the galleys of Mehmed Siroco, an adept Ottoman commander renowned for his naval tactics. Here, the sea churned with vigorous confrontations as each side sought to outflank and encircle the other.

Amid the tumult, moments of stunning bravery and sacrifice stood out. Christian soldiers boarded enemy ships with nothing but their swords and faith, facing the disciplined Janissaries, who were equally prepared to die for their sultan and their empire. These skirmishes, often brutal and decisive, began to influence the greater flow of battle as victories won on individual galleys contributed to the broader tactical picture.

The presence of religious symbols aboard the Christian ships served as a constant reminder of why they fought. The rosary beads grasped during quick prayers and the icons of saints mounted on masts provided a spiritual succor, a reassurance that their cause was just. The sacralized aura of the battlefield, where earthly combat met divine intercession, added a layer of transcendence to the physical struggle.

The initial hours of conflict saw no clear victor but set the stage for the epic confrontations that would follow. The first engagements at Lepanto were instrumental in determining the tactics and morale for the remainder of the battle. Each side, battered but unbroken, found itself locked in a deadly embrace, a testament to the resolve and ferocity of the combatants. Blood mixed with saltwater, sweat mingled with the scent of gunpowder, and the cries of the living and the dying became the soundtrack of this monumental clash.

Turning Points in the Battle

The Battle of Lepanto on October 7, 1571, was a momentous event that had several key turning points, each altering the tide of conflict. As the morning mist gave way to the rising sun, the two formidable fleets faced each other in the Gulf of Patras, their fates hanging in the balance.

One of the first pivotal moments occurred early on when the Christian fleet, under the command of Don Juan of Austria, decided to attack swiftly. The Ottoman fleet, commanded by Ali Pasha, had superior numbers, but the Christian commanders were well aware that speed and surprise could negate this advantage. With banners emblazoned with the image of Our Lady of Guadalupe fluttering in the wind and the Holy Rosary prayed fervently aboard the ships, morale was high among the Christian crews.

As the fleets drew closer, the initial skirmishes erupted into full-scale combat. The right wing of the Holy League, commanded by Venetian admiral Agostino Barbarigo, faced a significant challenge. They were up against the left wing of the Ottoman fleet, led by Mehmed Siroco. This fierce confrontation seemed evenly matched until the intervention of Andrea Doria's squadron. Doria, commanding the right wing reinforcement, managed to outflank the Ottoman positions, causing disarray and ultimately pushing them back. This maneuver was critical in maintaining the battle line's integrity and preventing an early breakthrough by the Ottomans.

Another turning point occurred at the heart of the conflict where Don Juan of Austria's flagship, the *Real*, clashed directly with Ali Pasha's *Sultana*. This duel was not just a battle of ships but a symbolic fight between the Christian and Islamic worlds. Both fleets had their elite troops engaged in vicious boarding actions. The intense hand-to-hand combat saw moments of bravery and desperation on both sides. Amidst this chaos, the death of Ali Pasha—a fateful wound delivered during the boarding fight—shattered Ottoman morale. His blood-stained turban, now a stark symbol of the shift in fortune, was raised as a trophy, signaling to both fleets that the Ottoman chain of command had been compromised.

On the left flank of the Christian fleet, commanded by Giovanni Andrea Doria, another critical moment unfolded. The Ottomans, under Uluc Ali, seized the opportunity to exploit a widening gap between Doria's forces and the central line. Uluc Ali and his forces aimed to isolate and surround segments of the Christian fleet. Realizing the potential disaster, Doria executed a tactical withdrawal, sacrificing some ground to re-establish a cohesive line. This tactical decision, although appearing as a retreat, succeeded in preventing encirclement and held the line together, averting a catastrophic defeat on that flank.

The deployment of the reserve fleet, under the command of the Marquess of Santa Cruz, proved to be another crucial factor. Seeing the unfolding chaos and recognizing the moments of opportunity, he brought in fresh ships to support the beleaguered sections of the Christian fleet. These reinforcements provided the necessary manpower and firepower to tip the scales. The reserves' entry into the fray not only bolstered the Christian line but delivered the essential counterattack that began to turn the battle's tide unequivocally in favor of the Holy League.

A defining aspect of the battle's turning points also lay in technological and tactical innovations. The Christians deployed several *galleasses,* heavily armed gunboats that laid down devastating broadsides before the main fleets engaged. These galleasses, stationed at strategic intervals, pounded the approaching Ottoman ships with relentless artillery fire. The destructive opening salvos from these vessels caused significant damage and lowered Ottoman morale before the close-quarters engagement began.

The relentless spiritual fervor also played an undeniably vital role. Throughout the battle, the sounds of muskets and cannons were interspersed with the prayers of men invoking the Virgin Mary, believed to be guiding them with divine intervention. The relentless recitation of the Rosary infused the Christian sailors and soldiers with a sense of purpose and spiritual fortitude, reinforcing their resolve during the most critical and dangerous moments of the battle.

The strategic use of fire ships by the Holy League was another momentous occurrence. These ships, filled with flammable materials, were set alight and directed towards the densely packed Ottoman vessels. The ensuing conflagration caused panic and disarray among the Ottoman sailors, further exacerbating their command and control issues, and leading to a chain reaction of chaos that eroded their fighting effectiveness.

The culmination of these efforts bore fruit as the afternoon sun illuminated the now-decisive shift in power. The Ottoman fleet began to fragment, and the overwhelming success of the Holy League's tactics and resilience became apparent. While pockets of fierce resistance continued, it was clear that the Ottoman cohesion had disintegrated. The remnants of Ali Pasha's fleet were either captured or set adrift, burning fiercely, marking the end of Ottoman naval supremacy in the Mediterranean.

By the time the sun dipped below the horizon, the battle had turned into a staggering victory for the Holy League. The significance of these turning points cannot be overstated. Each moment of bravery, each tactical insight, and every prayer recited contributed to the Christians' triumph. This victory did not just end a military engagement; it shifted the course of history, preventing the westward expansion of the Ottoman Empire and proving that determination, faith, and strategic brilliance could overcome overwhelming odds.

The Battle of Lepanto stands as a testament to the complex interplay of martial prowess, tactical decision-making, and spiritual conviction. As the smoke cleared and the victorious banners were raised, the echoes of the turning points resonated not just in the annals of history but in the hearts of those who believed their cause was just, their faith unwavering, and their victory foreordained.

The Final Clash

As the sun climbed higher above the horizon on October 7, 1571, the azure waters of the Gulf of Patras transformed into a theater of war. Don Juan of Austria's Christian fleet and the Ottoman armada, commanded by Ali Pasha, were locked in a deadly dance of naval combat. This was it—the moment that would seal the fate of the Mediterranean and determine which faith would hold sway over its waters. The morning's skirmishes had been bloody and relentless, setting an almost unbearable tension that coiled like a spring, ready to snap.

The Christian fleet's strategic arrangement, a formation known as the "crescent," had begun to show its effectiveness. The left wing, commanded by the Venetian Agostino Barbarigo, bore the brunt of the Ottoman attack. Barbarigo, despite sustaining a mortal wound, never faltered. His courage epitomized the unyielding spirit of the Holy League. Meanwhile, the Ottoman fleet, vast and formidable, maneuvered to encircle the Christians and overwhelm them with sheer numbers and firepower.

The heart of the Christian line, where Don Juan led aboard the Real, surged forth to meet Ali Pasha's Sultana. These two flagships symbolized more than mere vessels; they were the standard-bearers of Christendom and Islam. Cannons roared, and the air grew thick with smoke, obscuring the chaos as grappling hooks flew, connecting the ships in a deadly embrace. Swords clashed, and the cries of men echoed over the churning sea.

Just when it seemed the battle could tilt in favor of the Ottomans, a remarkable intervention occurred. The Christian League's reserve, led by the steadfast Gianandrea Doria, swung into action. Doria's galleys struck with precision, targeting the Ottoman flanks. The added strength bolstered the faltering Christian line, injecting fresh vigor into their assault.

As the afternoon sun climbed toward its zenith, the battle reached its critical juncture. The Real and Sultana had come so close that their crews could see the whites of each other's eyes. Ali Pasha's troops leapt aboard the Real in a frenzied attempt to capture Don Juan's flagship.

Hand-to-hand combat erupted on the decks, as both sides fought with a desperation only borne of existential conflict.

It was during these harrowing moments that fortune favored the bold. Marcantonio Colonna, another valiant commander of the Christian fleet, arrived with reinforcements. His well-timed intervention created an opportunity that Don Juan seized with fervor. The Christians rallied, pushing back the invaders. Amidst the turmoil, Ali Pasha was struck down, a death that sent shockwaves through the Ottoman forces.

The fall of Ali Pasha signaled a turning point. The once-unified Ottoman fleet began to fragment, its morale shattered by the loss of their leader. Don Juan's flagship surged forward, a beacon of victory now instead of a target. With renewed energy, the Christian forces pressed their advantage, driving the Ottomans into disarray.

Yet, even as hope kindled in the hearts of the Christians, they knew better than to underestimate their foe. The Ottoman soldiers fought with a ferocity born of their own convictions, their own duty. But the shattered command structure and the relentless Christian onslaught began to take its toll. Wounded and falling back, the Ottoman galleys tried to regroup but found themselves ensnared by the surrounding Christian ships.

As evening shadows lengthened, the outcome became inevitable. The Christian fleet had not merely survived; it had triumphed magnificently. On the decks of broken and burning vessels, men cried out in exhaustion and exultation. The banner of the Holy League fluttered triumphantly in the wind, a stark contrast to the smoke-laden air.

The losses were grievous on both sides, with the waters around Lepanto littered with the wreckage of ships and the bodies of fallen warriors. Despite the heavy price, the battle undeniably shifted the balance of power in the Mediterranean. The Ottomans, so long the scourge of Christian Europe, had been dealt a blow from which they would never fully recover.

This monumental clash was more than a mere military engagement; it was seen by many as a divine vindication. The victory was attributed not just to strategic brilliance or battlefield valor, but to the intercession of the divine—particularly through the Holy Rosary. The faithful believed that prayer had summoned celestial aid, turning the tide in favor of Christendom.

As tales of the victory spread throughout Europe, it became a rallying point for Christians everywhere, solidifying alliances and renewing religious fervor. The success at Lepanto did more than halt the Ottoman advance; it breathed new life into the Christian world, lifting spirits and hearts in a way that extended far beyond the battlefield.

The Battle of Lepanto, especially its climactic final clash, remains a potent symbol of faith, courage, and the power of divine intervention. It stands as a testament to the resilience and unity achievable when people are driven by a higher purpose, and as a pivotal moment that shaped the course of history in the Mediterranean and beyond.

Chapter 8: Key Personalities in the Battle

The Battle of Lepanto was a fierce and decisive conflict that brought to the forefront some of the era's most significant figures. Central among them was Don Juan of Austria, the charismatic and skilled commander of the Holy League, whose leadership turned the tides in favor of the Christian fleet. Opposing him was the formidable Ottoman admiral, Ali Pasha, known for his strategic acumen and unyielding resolve. Alongside these two titans stood notable warriors and commanders on both sides, whose bravery and tactical genius were instrumental in the course of the battle. Their collective efforts and sacrifices not only shaped the outcome of Lepanto but also left an indelible mark on the annals of history, serving as a testament to the pivotal roles individuals play in the grand tapestry of human events.

Don Juan of Austria

Don Juan of Austria remains one of the most compelling figures in the annals of European history. Born in Regensburg on February 24,

1547, as a so-called "natural" son of Holy Roman Emperor Charles V, his lineage might suggest a life shadowed by repudiation and obscurity. Instead, Don Juan would rise to be the luminous commander at the Battle of Lepanto, an epic clash that halted the Ottoman advance into Christian Europe.

The early days of Don Juan's life were marked by relative anonymity. His mother, Barbara Blomberg, a German burgher's daughter, would see her son taken from her care and placed under the tutelage of Luis de Quijada, a loyal servant to the emperor. Yet, by the age of seven, the young Juan was sent to live in the court of his half-brother, Philip II of Spain. There, he was educated under the covert title of "Jerónimo" to safeguard his identity. As he grew, his martial inclinations and natural intuition for leadership began to surface, traits that would soon serve Christendom in its hour of need.

Don Juan's ascension in the military ranks was swift and marked by a series of impressive achievements. Named General of the Mediterranean Fleet at the tender age of twenty-four, he displayed a prowess and wisdom far beyond his years. During the revolt in the Alpujarras, the young commander exhibited exceptional courage and tactical brilliance, gaining the confidence of King Philip II. This trust would soon place him at the helm of the Holy League's fleet, an assemblage of ships from Spain, Venice, and the Papal States, united under the auspices of Pope Pius V to resist Ottoman expansion.

The Battle of Lepanto on October 7, 1571, arguably forms the pinnacle of Don Juan's career. Mustering a force of over 200 galleys, he led his men into a confrontation with the Ottoman fleet, a formidable force led by Ali Pasha. Under ominous skies, the azure waters of the Gulf of Patras would become a theater of war, echoing with the sound of cannon fire and clashing swords. Don Juan's command style was both inspirational and direct. Insisting on positioning himself centrally in the fray, his flagship, the "Real," served as both a literal and symbolic heart of the Christian forces.

Determined to counter the Ottoman might, his strategy and leadership became pivotal. Don Juan's battle plan, which involved arraying the Holy League's fleet in a broad crescent to counter the enemy's crescent formation, epitomized his tactical astuteness. He capitalized on the superior maneuverability of his galleasses and utilized the wind and sun to the fleet's advantage. As the morning sun ascended, it cast a blinding glare on the Ottoman forces, stymieing their advance and enhancing the strategic position of Don Juan's armada.

The battle was characterized by brutal close-quarters combat. Don Juan himself led boarding parties, sword in hand, exemplifying the knightly virtues of valor and gallantry. In the midst of the chaos, his presence invigorated his men, attesting to the magnetic leadership that held the coalition together. The eventual capture of Ali Pasha's flagship and the visible decapitation of the enemy leader marked a decisive turning point, signaling a catastrophic defeat for the Ottomans and a resounding victory for the Christian forces.

Don Juan's exemplary leadership at Lepanto had ramifications that extended well beyond the immediate military triumph. Symbolically, he became the paladin of Christian Europe, embodying the collective aspirations of a continent beleaguered by Ottoman incursions. His success reinvigorated the morale of Christendom, inspiring countless artworks, poems, and songs that celebrated this momentous victory. In a broader context, his legacy as a defender of the faith and a strategic genius would be memorialized in numerous historical records.

Post-Lepanto, Don Juan continued to be a pivotal figure in European and Mediterranean politics. Appointed as Governor-General of the Spanish Netherlands in 1576, his tenure was marked by attempts to stabilize the region fraught with religious and political tensions. However, his later years were less illustrious, defined by festering tensions with Philip II and deteriorating health. Despite these challenges, Don Juan's reputation as the "Most Catholic Prince" remained unblemished, his name forever entwined with the victory that preserved the Christian West from Ottoman domination.

In closing, Don Juan of Austria stands as a quintessential figure in the great tapestry of the Battle of Lepanto. His life, steeped in both legend and history, offers an enduring testament to the power of divine providence and human valor. From his humble beginnings to his rise as a military commander, his journey encapsulates the quintessence of knightly heroism. His story serves not only as a historical account but as an epic narrative that continues to resonate through the ages, affirming the ideals of courage, faith, and unwavering leadership in the face of insurmountable odds.

Ali Pasha

To understand the Battle of Lepanto, one must grasp the formidable role played by Ali Pasha, the commanding force behind the Ottoman fleet. Born Mehmet Shaban in 1500 in the distinctly multicultural city of Pirlepe, he emerged from the complexities of the Balkan lands, characterized by a gripping interlacing of cultures, religions, and tumultuous histories. Ali Pasha, later renamed Müezzinzade Ali Pasha, navigated his path to preeminence through a blend of military expertise and sagacity, becoming an epitome of Ottoman ambition and naval prowess.

Ali Pasha's rise in the Ottoman hierarchy was astoundingly swift. Initially groomed within the devshirme system, where Christian boys were recruited and converted to serve the sultan, he demonstrated his military acumen early on. His notable success in quelling rebellions and defending the empire's maritime domains granted him not only the coveted position of Kapudan Pasha, the Grand Admiral but also immense trust from Sultan Selim II. Ali Pasha's career became a testament to the meritocratic elements within the Ottoman administrative machine.

As the commander of the fabled Ottoman armada, Ali Pasha was entrusted with maintaining Ottoman supremacy in the Mediterranean, a sea crucial for the geopolitical equilibrium of the time. His strategic outlook was sharpened by numerous encounters with European foes, and his fleet was both a symbol of Ottoman dominance and a veritable force of devastation. Under his aegis, the Ottoman naval forces were meticulously prepared for engagements, fully equipped with state-of-the-art weaponry, and driven by the indomitable spirit of expansion.

The Ottoman empire, flourishing under Sultan Selim II, was at its zenith of naval strength and territorial expanse. Ali Pasha had been meticulously appointed to command the Ottoman fleet at Lepanto, a choice illustrating the gravity with which the Ottoman leadership viewed the forthcoming confrontation. The rendezvous at Lepanto was not merely a clash of military forces but a battle imbued with religio-political undertones, and Ali Pasha stood as the personification of Islamic resistance against the encroaching Christian coalition.

Interestingly, the Battle of Lepanto was characterized by an unusual level of chivalric courtesy between adversaries, even amidst the intense ferocity of combat. Ali Pasha, knowing the stakes, inspired his men with both fervor and personal bravery. Accounts reveal that he carried a copy of the Qur'an into battle, an emblem of his piety and an exhortation for divine favor and protection. This spiritual dimension mirrored the Holy Rosary's significance for the Christian forces, rendering the conflict a true confrontation of faiths.

In the heat of battle, Ali Pasha's leadership was both decisive and ferocious. He directed his fleet from the Sultana, his flagship, and led from the front, embodying the valor and determination that had long epitomized the Ottoman commanders. The initial phases of the battle saw the Ottoman fleet gaining ground, bolstered by their superior numbers and advantageous positions. Ali Pasha's tactical decisions early on reflected his deep understanding of naval engagements, grounded in both classical strategies and innovative maneuvers.

Yet, as the battle wore on, the resolve of the Holy League, coupled with divine intercessions as many believed, tilted the scales. Crucial turning points, such as the engagement with Don Juan of Austria's flagship, the Real, tested Ali Pasha's command. Reports indicate that Ali Pasha fought valiantly till his final breath. Despite the overwhelming force arrayed against him, he resisted capture or execution, choosing instead to embrace martyrdom.

Ali Pasha's death marked a significant turning point in the Battle of Lepanto. His beheading and the loss of the Sultana devastated Ottoman morale, leading to a chaotic retreat. The symbolic resonance of his demise was enormous; it heralded the crumbling of Ottoman supremacy in the Mediterranean for a time and emphasized the fragile nature of even the mightiest empires. His fall became a narrative of valor and tragedy, deeply impacting both Islamic and Christian chronicles of the event.

The historical legacy of Ali Pasha is multifaceted. To some, he epitomizes the relentless spirit and grandeur of the Ottoman Empire, and to others, he is a cautionary tale of the perils entailed in imperial overreach. His role at Lepanto, dissected by numerous historians and strategists over subsequent centuries, offers invaluable insights into the intricacies of leadership, the capricious nature of warfare, and the profound impact of individual will and bravery on the course of history.

Ali Pasha's inclusion in the annals of the Battle of Lepanto is indispensable. His life, marked by devout piety and war, provides a compelling narrative inextricably linked to the larger tapestry of East-West conflicts during the Renaissance. As such, his story enriches the historical discourse on Lepanto, offering lessons and reflections that reverberate through the corridors of time and continue to captivate the imaginations of Roman Catholics, strategists, and historians alike.

Notable Warriors and Commanders

Among the rich tapestry of the Battle of Lepanto, the figures that stand out most vividly are those of the warriors and commanders. These individuals, through a combination of valor, strategic acumen, and divine inspiration, shaped the course of this monumental naval clash and left an indelible mark on history. Their spirits embodied the ethos of the time, intertwining faith and warfare in a manner that still resonates in the hearts and minds of believers and historians alike.

Don Juan of Austria, the half-brother of King Philip II of Spain, emerged as one of the most prominent figures among the Christian forces. At the tender age of 24, he was entrusted with an immense responsibility, leading the Holy League's fleet against the formidable Ottoman armada. His leadership was characterized by a blend of youthful zeal and mature strategic insight. Eyewitness accounts often highlight his ability to inspire and unify disparate factions within the alliance, a testament to his charisma and statesmanship. It was under his command that the Christian fleet saw its aspirations transform into a resounding victory.

Ali Pasha, the high-ranking Ottoman commander, was another key figure whose presence dominated the historical narrative of the Battle of Lepanto. A seasoned warrior with a keen sense of naval tactics, Ali Pasha was the orchestrator of the Ottoman fleet. His experience and reputation instilled confidence and loyalty amongst his men. Despite the eventual outcome, his strategies and counter-strategies during the battle showcased his ingenuity and resourcefulness, solidifying his place as a notable commander in the annals of military history.

Alongside these colossal figures were countless other warriors and commanders whose actions, though perhaps less documented, were equally pivotal. One such individual was Agostino Barbarigo, the Venetian captain-general. Tasked with commanding the left wing of the Holy League's fleet, Barbarigo displayed exceptional bravery and tactical prowess. His leadership was instrumental in repelling the initial onslaught by the Ottoman forces, and though he ultimately succumbed to his wounds, his contributions paved the way for the ultimate victory.

Marco Antonio Colonna, commanding the center of the Holy League's fleet alongside Don Juan, brought with him a wealth of experience from his previous military campaigns. His role in maintaining the cohesion and discipline of the fleet cannot be overstated. Colonna's tactical decisions during the heat of battle proved critical, particularly in the face of Ali Pasha's aggressive maneuvers. His coordination with Don Juan exemplified the efficacy of collaborative leadership in achieving a common goal.

On the Ottoman side, Murad Bey and Uluç Ali stand out as formidable commanders who fought valiantly against the Christian forces.

Murad Bey, commanding the Ottoman right wing, demonstrated relentless determination and resilience, traits that inspired his men to hold their ground even as the tide of battle turned against them. Uluç Ali, known for his exceptional naval skills and cunning, managed to evade capture and later played a significant role in the Ottoman naval rebuilding efforts post-Lepanto.

The contributions of these warriors and commanders extend beyond the battlefield; their actions had far-reaching implications for their respective empires and the broader geopolitical landscape. Don Juan's victory bolstered the morale of Christian Europe and asserted naval dominance in the Mediterranean, while Ali Pasha's defeat marked a turning point for the Ottoman Empire, necessitating a reevaluation of their maritime strategies.

The interplay of these leadership figures highlights the complexity and multifaceted nature of the Battle of Lepanto. Each commander brought unique strengths and perspectives, yet it was the convergence of their efforts, both adversarial and allied, that created the historic tapestry of this battle. Their legacies serve as a testament to the intricate dynamics of war, illustrating how individual valor and decision-making coalesce with larger strategic objectives.

From a broader historical and theological perspective, the roles of these key figures are often seen through the lens of providence and divine intervention. The Catholic Church, in particular, views the victory at Lepanto as a manifestation of divine favor, a narrative intertwined with the invocation of the Holy Rosary by Pope Pius V. This spiritual dimension adds another layer to the understanding of these commanders' contributions, elevating their military achievements within the wider context of faith and divine will.

Moreover, the chronicling of their endeavors provides invaluable insights into the leadership qualities and tactical innovations of the period. Modern strategists and historians draw upon these accounts to glean lessons on command efficacy, coalition warfare, and the interplay between technology and human ingenuity in naval engagements. The Battle of Lepanto, through the prism of its notable warriors and commanders, continues to serve as a rich case study in the enduring principles of military strategy and leadership.

As we delve deeper into the narratives of these figures, it becomes evident that their stories are not just about victory or defeat but about the embodiment of virtues such as courage, faith, and resilience. They remind us of the human capacity to strive for ideals greater than oneself, to lead with conviction, and to persevere against formidable odds. It is through their lives and legacies that we gain a deeper appreciation of the historical significance of the Battle of Lepanto.

The interplay of military strategy and divine inspiration in the actions of these commanders also mirrors the broader cultural and religious milieu of the time. It reflects a world where temporal and spiritual realms were inextricably linked, influencing decisions on the battlefield and beyond. The enduring legacy of these notable warriors and commanders, therefore, lies not only in their tactical acumen but also in their embodiment of a worldview that saw the hand of providence in the course of human events.

Ultimately, the stories of Don Juan of Austria, Ali Pasha, and their fellow warriors and commanders are woven into the larger narrative of the Battle of Lepanto, a narrative that continues to captivate and inspire. Their actions, driven by a blend of personal valor and strategic vision, played a crucial role in shaping the outcome of the battle and, by extension, the course of history. As we reflect on their contributions, we are reminded of the profound impact that individual leaders can have on the tides of history, an impact that resonates across centuries and continues to inform our understanding of leadership, faith, and warfare.

Chapter 9: The Role of the Holy Rosary

The Holy Rosary emerged as a potent tool of faith and perseverance during the critical moments of the Battle of Lepanto, weaving its spiritual significance through the lives of countless devout Christians. St. Pius V, ardently devoted to the Virgin Mary, called upon Christendom to unite in prayer, invoking the Rosary to seek divine intervention against the formidable Ottoman fleet. The rhythmic cadence of the prayers echoed across Europe, fostering a collective resilience and a shared hope that transcended geographical and political divides. On the day of the battle, October 7, 1571, the Christian fleet, bolstered by a sense of divine favor, engaged their adversaries with unyielding courage. Historians argue that the palpable morale among the forces was not merely militaristic but profoundly spiritual, galvanized by the Rosary's promise of victory and protection. This confluence of faith and strategy revealed the Rosary's integral role, not just as a devotional object, but as a symbol of unity and divine providence, culminating in a triumph that reshaped the historical destiny of Christendom.

Origins and Significance

The Holy Rosary, a string of beads that leads the faithful through a series of prayers, possesses roots that delve deep into ancient Christian traditions and the spiritual practices of early religious communities. While its exact beginnings are enshrouded in the mists of history, the origins of the Rosary can be traced back to the early monastic communities of the desert fathers, who used knotted cords to keep track of their prayers. Over the centuries, these cords evolved into the structured form of the Rosary we recognize today, a transformation that speaks volumes about the enduring need for a physical tool to guide and discipline prayer.

The significance of the Rosary is multifaceted, enveloping both personal devotion and communal solidarity. For many Roman Catholics, the Rosary serves as a potent spiritual exercise, a means by which they can meditate on key events in the lives of Jesus and Mary. These events, or "mysteries," are categorized into Joyful, Sorrowful, Glorious, and, more recently, Luminous Mysteries, each offering a deeper dive into the foundational moments of Christian faith. Through the repetition of prayers, the Rosary centers the heart and mind, creating a rhythm that mirrors the heartbeat, fostering a spiritual connection that transcends the mundane.

Historically, the introduction and propagation of the Rosary have been attributed to Saint Dominic in the 13th century. According to tradition, the Virgin Mary appeared to him and gave him the Rosary as a means to combat heresy and bring people back to the faith. Whether this account is taken literally or symbolically, it underscores the Rosary's role as a spiritual weapon in the battle against evil and error. The Dominican Order, with its emphasis on preaching and teaching, played a crucial role in spreading the recitation of the Rosary, positioning it as an integral part of Catholic piety.

Moreover, the Rosary stands as a testament to the relational nature of Catholic spirituality. It reflects the belief in intercessory prayer—turning to Mary and the saints to intercede with God on one's behalf. This belief is deeply rooted in the Catholic understanding of the Communion of Saints, a spiritual solidarity that transcends time and space. The repetitive prayers of the Rosary create a sense of unity among the faithful, connecting individuals not only with God but also with each other, forming a communal chain of prayer that spans the globe.

The strategic significance of the Rosary became evident in pivotal historical moments, particularly during the Battle of Lepanto in 1571. As the Ottoman Empire threatened to overrun Christian Europe, Pope Pius V called for a Rosary crusade, urging the faithful to pray for victory. The subsequent triumph of the Holy League at Lepanto was attributed to this collective prayer effort, cementing the Rosary's reputation as a powerful weapon against overwhelming odds. The Rosary, therefore, not only molds personal faith but also galvanizes communal action in times of crisis.

The victory at Lepanto was considered miraculous, a divine endorsement of the power of communal prayer through the Rosary. Following this victory, Pope Pius V instituted the Feast of Our Lady of Victory, later renamed the Feast of Our Lady of the Rosary, to commemorate the role of the Rosary in this pivotal event. This feast serves as an annual reminder of the Rosary's significance, celebrating its capacity to unite and strengthen the faithful in the face of formidable challenges.

In a broader cultural context, the Rosary has influenced numerous aspects of Catholic life and liturgy. It has inspired countless works of art, literature, and music, each exploring the depths of its spiritual and historical significance. The visual depictions of the Rosary in paintings and sculptures often reflect its role as a bridge between the sacred and the secular, illustrating the profound impact of this simple string of beads on the collective Catholic consciousness.

Furthermore, the practice of reciting the Rosary is embedded in various Catholic traditions and rituals. It is often recited in groups during special occasions, processions, and vigils, fostering a sense of communal spirituality. The Rosary's role in these gatherings underscores its function as both a personal and a public expression of faith, linking individual devotion with collective worship.

In modern times, the Rosary continues to hold a special place in the hearts of many Catholics. Amidst the distractions and chaos of contemporary life, it offers a sanctuary of peace and reflection, a momentary retreat into the sacred. The Rosary's enduring appeal lies in its simplicity and depth—it is accessible to all, yet invites profound meditation on the mysteries of faith. It is a spiritual practice that adapts to the needs of the time while retaining its timeless essence.

The Rosary also serves as a unifying force among Catholics worldwide. Despite cultural and linguistic differences, the basic structure and prayers of the Rosary remain consistent, fostering a sense of global solidarity. This unity is particularly evident during international events such as World Youth Day, where thousands of young Catholics come together to pray the Rosary, transcending barriers and affirming their shared faith.

Educationally, the Rosary offers a unique opportunity for catechesis, providing a framework for teaching the core beliefs and stories of Christianity. Through the mysteries, the faithful are guided through the Gospel narrative, gaining insights into the life, death, and resurrection of Jesus Christ. The meditative nature of the Rosary also encourages deeper reflection and understanding, nurturing a more intimate relationship with God.

The Rosary's significance extends beyond its religious implications, influencing social and political spheres as well. Throughout history, numerous leaders and movements have turned to the Rosary for guidance and inspiration. For instance, the Rosary played a pivotal role during tumultuous periods such as the Polish Solidarity movement, underscoring its capacity to inspire hope and resilience in the face of adversity.

Ultimately, the Rosary is a testament to the enduring power of prayer and the unbreakable bond between faith and action. Its origins, steeped in tradition and history, and its profound significance, both personal and communal, render it a cornerstone of Catholic spirituality. As the faithful continue to navigate the challenges of the modern world, the Rosary remains a constant source of strength, solace, and spiritual renewal.

The Rosary and the Battle

The Battle of Lepanto, fought on October 7, 1571, holds a unique place in the annals of history, not just for its military significance but also for the profound spiritual elements that underscored it. The formidable clash between the Ottoman Empire and the Holy League was perceived by many contemporaries as a decisive confrontation between Christianity and Islam. However, it's the role of the Holy Rosary in this monumental event that continues to fascinate and inspire generations of Catholics and historians alike.

Weeks before the fleets clashed in the Gulf of Patras, Pope Pius V called upon all Christians to pray the Holy Rosary for the victory of the Holy League. It wasn't merely a battle strategy; it was a call to spiritual arms. The Pope, a fervent believer in the intercessory power of the Blessed Virgin Mary, saw the Rosary as a potent weapon in a time of imminent threat. This profound act of faith turned the Rosary into more than beads strung together on a cord; it became a symbol of unity, hope, and divine intervention.

As the dawn of October 7 unfolded, sailors aboard the Christian ships held their rosaries tightly, invoking the intercession of Our Lady. The atmosphere, tense with apprehension and anticipation, was imbued with a solemn sense of piety. Men who typically wielded swords and muskets now clutched rosary beads, their lips moving in fervent prayer. This collective act of devotion wasn't merely for show; it had deep roots in the belief that victory was not solely in human hands but also rested in divine will.

It's worth noting that the Rosary, with its structure of repeated prayers, offers a meditative cadence that can bring a profound sense of peace and focus. That day, the rhythmic recitation of the Rosary may have provided the sailors with a sense of calm and steadiness amidst the dread of impending battle. Such spiritual grounding was crucial for men facing the enormity and brutality of naval warfare. The divine influence they sought through prayer gave them courage and bolstered their resolve.

When the battle began, it was fierce and chaotic. Canon fire roared, and ships clashed with the tumult of hand-to-hand combat. Despite the fury of the physical battle, accounts suggest a palpable sense of divine presence. Midway through the clash, the tide turned favorably for the Holy League, a turn of events attributed by many to the intervention of the Virgin Mary. The resulting Christian victory was perceived not just as a military triumph but as a vindication of their faith.

Authors and historians have long debated the tangible impact of the Holy Rosary on the outcome of the Battle of Lepanto. Was it the strategic prowess of Don Juan of Austria, the youthful and charismatic leader of the Holy League, that clinched the victory? Or was it the prayers of thousands that swayed divine favor? While we may never have empirical answers, the intertwining of faith and history at Lepanto is undeniable.

In the wake of the victory, Pope Pius V established the Feast of Our Lady of Victory, later renamed the Feast of Our Lady of the

Rosary. This annual celebration continues to honor the belief that it was through the Rosary's intercessory power that the Holy League achieved such an improbable victory. The feast serves as a reminder of the battle and the spiritual heritage that underscored it, keeping alive the memory of prayer's power in times of crisis.

The devotion to the Holy Rosary surged after Lepanto, embedding itself deeper into the fabric of Catholic spirituality. The victory reinforced the Rosary's reputation as not just a tool for personal meditation but as a communal bond and a spiritual weapon in the face of adversity. From that point on, the Rosary was often linked with hope, resilience, and divine intercession, themes that have echoed over the centuries and across different struggles that the faithful have faced.

Moreover, the spiritual narrative of the Battle of Lepanto contributes to its epic stature. Here were seasoned sailors and warriors, bowing their heads in prayer, placing their trust in a higher power as cannons loomed and enemy ships bore down upon them. This juxtaposition of martial ferocity and devout spirituality creates a tableau that is extraordinarily compelling. It embodies the synthesis of human endeavor and divine reliance, a theme resonant with Catholics and historians alike.

Therefore, to fully grasp the significance of the Battle of Lepanto, one must appreciate the pivotal role that the Holy Rosary played. This is not a mere footnote to military strategy but a fundamental aspect of the event's narrative. The Holy Rosary served as the conduit through which the divine was beseeched for intervention, altering the course of history through the combined power of faith and action. The Battle of Lepanto, set against the broader tapestry of the military and spiritual history, affirms the profound belief that, in moments of dire peril, the recourse of the faithful can wield extraordinary influence.

The reverberations of this belief continue to inspire. The enduring power of the Rosary, forged in the crucible of battle, has become an emblem of hope and divine perseverance. For Roman Catholics today, it serves as a testament to the enduring efficacy of prayer and the continuous call to unite in faith, especially in times of trial. Strategists and historians, while examining the tactical and political ramifications of Lepanto, also acknowledge the undeniable spirit that animated its participants.

In the end, understanding "The Rosary and the Battle" is essential for a comprehensive grasp of the Battle of Lepanto. It reveals the intricate dance between faith and strategy, between human effort and divine intervention. It tells us that the victories of the flesh are often intertwined with the triumphs of the spirit and that the Holy Rosary will forever remain a symbol of this extraordinary fusion. As we reflect on Lepanto, we do so not just in terms of ships and strategy, but with a recognition of the profound spiritual dimensions that shaped it and continue to inspire us.

Chapter 10: The Miracle of the Holy House

The Miracle of the Holy House stands as a profound testament to divine intervention and the intertwining of sacred history with the pivotal Battle of Lepanto. According to long-held tradition, the Holy House of Loreto, believed to be the very dwelling where the Virgin Mary received the Annunciation, was miraculously transported by angels from Nazareth to Loreto, Italy, in 1294. This sacred structure not only became a revered pilgrimage site but also served as a spiritual bulwark for the Christian forces. On the eve of the Battle of Lepanto, the invocation of the Virgin of Loreto and the recitation of the Holy Rosary galvanized the Christian fleet, imbuing them with a sense of divine mission. Eyewitness accounts detail how an extraordinary vision of the Holy House appeared in the sky, bolstering the morale of the outnumbered Christians and leading them to an improbable yet decisive victory. This miraculous event was seen as a tangible affirmation of heavenly favor, aligning the earthly struggle with a higher, celestial purpose, and cementing the Holy House's significance in both faith and history.

Accounts of the Miracle

The accounts of the miracle surrounding the Holy House of Loreto are as vast as they are fascinating. Originating in Nazareth, this small edifice had reportedly been the dwelling of the Virgin Mary and Jesus Christ. At the heart of these accounts lies the enigmatic translation of the Holy House from the Holy Land to its current sanctuary in Loreto, Italy. The sheer audacity and mystical nature of this event have captivated the imaginations of both the devout and the skeptical for centuries.

One of the most striking accounts comes from the late 13th century when the house is said to have been miraculously transported by angels. According to these narratives, in 1291, as Muslim forces advanced into the Holy Land, angels lifted the sacred house and carried it first to modern-day Croatia, and three years later to Italy. This astounding tale spread rapidly, bolstered by the testimonies of those who claimed to have witnessed the miraculous journey.

One ecclesiastical chronicler recounts that upon arriving in Loreto, the house was found to fit precisely onto a foundation that seemed prepared for it, despite the apparent randomness of its chosen location. This account has been interpreted by many as a sign of divine preordination, an element that underscores the belief in the miraculous nature of the house's arrival.

Documentary evidence from contemporary sources, including Papal bulls and other ecclesiastical writings, further substantiates these traditions. Pope Urban VI and Pope Clement VII endorsed the authenticity of the Holy House. Such endorsements added an ecclesiastical weight to the accounts, encouraging pilgrims to visit the site. These accounts form a vital chapter in the devotional literature surrounding Loreto, offering a historical and theological context for the House's presence in Italy.

A multitude of miracles reportedly occurred in the vicinity of the Holy House soon after its arrival in Loreto. These range from miraculous healings to visions and inexplicable lights seen by the faithful. Pilgrims would flock to Loreto, seeking solace, miracles, and a touch of the divine. One famous account details how a paralyzed man, upon touching the walls of the Holy House, found himself immediately healed, walking away with tears of gratitude.

Beyond individual testimonies, there are also physical remnants and artifacts attesting to the Holy House's journey. For instance, stones from the original foundation in Nazareth bear remarkable similarity to those in Loreto. Archaeological examinations and historical comparisons have lent a degree of credence to the idea that the Holy House did, indeed, originate in the Holy Land.

One may not ignore the profound influence of the Holy House during the period leading up to the Battle of Lepanto. As the Christian forces prepared to face the Ottoman Empire, they believed the Holy House stood as a beacon of divine favor. Pope Pius V invoked the protection of the Virgin Mary, whose earthly home now stood in Loreto, rallying the Christian armies under her aegis.

Intrepid chroniclers and historians documented the surge in morale among Christian soldiers who visited Loreto. They attested to a divine presence that bolstered their courage. It is said that the Holy House was instrumental in forging a spiritual alliance among the fractious European powers, unifying them under a common sacred cause. The miracle of Loreto thus imbued the Holy League's mission with an almost holy crusade-like fervor.

The accounts of scholars and theologians also emphasize the Holy House's role as a theological symbol. For example, it was cited as an embodiment of the Incarnation—God becoming man and dwelling among us. The house, in this sense, became a tangible representation of divine mystery, a cornerstone of Marian devotion and Christological symbolism. Throughout the centuries, theologians have pondered the implications of this miracle, enriching Mariology and deepening spiritual reflections about the Virgin Mary's role in salvation history.

As with all miraculous claims, skepticism and critical inquiries have also arisen. Yet, the resilience of the accounts through various trials and the inexplicable elements involved have kept the mystery alive. Even the skeptics find themselves grappling with unanswered questions about the origins and continued veneration of the Holy House.

Liturgical acknowledgment of the miracle has played a significant role in its preservation and reverence. Pope Benedict XIV, in the 18th century, confirmed the traditional belief that the Holy House of Loreto was the same house in which the Annunciation occurred. This papal acknowledgment fortified the belief in its miraculous journey and anchored it firmly within Church tradition.

For historians and strategists, the story of the Holy House offers more than just a tale of divine intervention. It presents an intriguing case of how faith and historical events intersect. The legend of the angels ferrying the Holy House might first appear fantastical, yet it nonetheless served to galvanize Catholic Europe at a critical juncture. By setting a tangible sacred space in Italy, it inspired plots and counterplots, pilgrimages, and political maneuverings. The Holy House became an incontrovertible asset to the Christian cause, a living testament to divine favor crucial during the turbulent times of the Ottoman threat.

Indeed, the Holy House and its miracle provided a rallying point, not only for the faithful but also for the political and military strategists who recognized the importance of morale and divine endorsement. In many ways, the accounts of the miracle served as a unifying mythos, harnessing both spiritual and temporal power to combat a common enemy.

In summarizing the myriad accounts of the miracle, what stands out is the blend of history, faith, and myth. The miraculous transfer of the Holy House from Nazareth to Loreto remains one of the most celebrated events in Catholic tradition. It captivates not just the pious but also those who study the interplay of divine narratives within the tapestry of history. Whether viewed through the lens of faith or the scrutiny of historical analysis, the accounts of the Holy House of Loreto endure, a testament to the profound and mysterious ways in which divine providence is believed to act in the world.

Its Role in the Battle

Amidst the myriad of factors contributing to the triumphant outcome at the Battle of Lepanto, the Holy House of Loreto's celestial role stands as a cornerstone of divine intercession. The very notion of the Holy House—the dwelling where the Blessed Virgin is believed to have dwelt and which was miraculously transported from Nazareth to Loreto—resonated profoundly among the Christian forces. This sanctuary became both a spiritual bastion and a symbol of heavenly protection, an embodiment of the divine favor that Christians perceived in their struggle against the formidable Ottoman Empire.

The Christian sailors and soldiers, embarking on this perilous campaign, carried with them the hope and fervor that emanated from their devotion to the Holy House. The disjointed solidarity among the European powers found unity and purpose in their shared veneration of this sacred site. While varied in language and culture, every man was tethered to the promise of divine assistance that the Holy House represented. Pilgrims frequented Loreto, seeking not just physical proximity but spiritual fortitude for the coming battle. This collective seeking of grace transformed individual strengths into a formidable force, ready to counter the advancing Ottoman fleet.

Moreover, the prayers offered at the Holy House were regarded as direct petitions to the Blessed Virgin for a miraculous intervention. On the eve of battle, a sense of elevated purpose and divine mission pervaded the Christian camps. These prayers, echoed in the vast waters separating the two formidable navies, served as a binding force that supplanted fear with unyielding faith. Leaders, warriors, and common sailors alike felt an invisible hand guiding their efforts, a protective mantle over their cause. This shift from mere mortal combatants to instruments of divine will played a fundamental role in their resilience and valor.

Adding an epic layer to this narrative was the role of Pope Saint Pius V, who orchestrated a network of prayer and supplication. He urged the faithful across Christendom to seek the intercession of Our Lady of Loreto, invoking her aid through the Holy Rosary. The synergy of these prayers, centralized on the Holy House, created a spiritual fortress as impassable as any physical stronghold. In cities and villages far removed from the theater of war, the laity gathered to support the naval forces, their supplications rising like incense and fortifying the warriors at Lepanto.

These prayers bore an undeniable fruit on the battlefield. As the conflict reached its fiercest points, many eyewitnesses recounted visions of Our Lady, her presence perceived as an assuring signal of victory. The valor witnessed among the Christian fleets transcended typical explanations of mere human courage. Emboldened by a sense of divine mission, the warriors witnessed strokes of improbable fortune and displays of unity that bore the signatures of miraculous intervention. Strategically, their cohesive maneuvers showcased brilliance that seemed, at times, otherworldly, underpinned by the blessing associated with the Holy House.

The central role of the Holy House in the Battle of Lepanto isn't merely anecdotal or legendary; it was formally acknowledged by ecclesiastical figures and chroniclers of the age. In the words of contemporary historians, the Holy House served as a 'beacon of hope', channeling divine insight and strength into the hearts of those who defended the Christian world. The sanctuary's connection to the Blessed Virgin rendered it an unearthly command center from which grace was deployed as effectively as any ship or cannon. Warriors saw this not solely as a physical struggle but as a metaphysical confrontation between good and evil, a holy war underlined by the sanctity of Loreto.

Beyond the immediate battlefield dynamics, the cultural and theological implications of the Holy House's involvement left an enduring legacy on Christian Europe. Victories attributed to divine intervention fostered a renaissance of faith, strengthening clerical and laical bonds. Churches dedicated to Our Lady of Loreto sprung up across the continent, embodying the spirit of victory and divine favor in stone and mortar. Theological treatises of the period explored the nuances of this intervention, further embedding the Holy House's role into the spiritual and cultural matrix of the time.

The battle's outcome also revitalized the doctrine of intercessory prayer within the Catholic tradition. The faithful, now more than ever, recognized the tangible power of the divine in temporal affairs. This was a defining moment, reinforcing the concept that earthly battles, when fought under the imprimatur of heavenly patronage, could yield victories that streets, swords, and ships alone would find elusive. The Holy House stood as a testament to this communion, a cornerstone of intercession in the grandiose narrative of history.

This interweaving of the sacred and the martial marked a unique chapter in both the annals of military strategy and ecclesiastical history. The two realms, often perceived as distinct, revealed a potent alchemy when brought together under the auspices of faith. The narrative of the Holy House in relation to the Battle of Lepanto exemplified this synthesis, an odyssey where divine resonance reshaped the tactical landscapes of human endeavor.

In examining the interplay between the Holy House and the climactic victory at Lepanto, it's pivotal to understand that this wasn't an isolated phenomenon but a continuum in the grand tapestry of the Church's history. Each subsequent victory and defeat carried echoes from this seminal moment, the Blessed Virgin's intercession at Loreto continuing to embolden the faithful across generations. Strategists and militarists would do well to acknowledge how spiritual dynamics can interplay with martial tactics, as the Holy House's role in the Battle of Lepanto so profoundly illustrates.

Thus, in the grand confluence of faith, strategy, and martial might, the blessing of the Holy House of Loreto carved its indelible mark on the Battle of Lepanto. The Holy House, a nexus of divine grace and human valor, stood as a bulwark of hope and did not merely influence, but rather, was integral to the Christian triumph. Through the prayers offered within its sacred precincts, it channeled divine intervention directly onto the turbulent waters of Lepanto, transforming the course of history in favor of the Christian forces, and establishing an everlasting testament to the power of faith and divine intercession.

Chapter 11: The Feast of Our Lady of Victory

The Feast of Our Lady of Victory, established by Pope Pius V in thanksgiving for the miraculous triumph at the Battle of Lepanto, stands as a testament to the power of faith and divine intercession. Celebrated on October 7th, this feast day has been enshrined in the liturgical calendar as a reminder of the pivotal moment when the Christian forces, through prayer and the invocation of the Holy Rosary, overcame the seemingly invincible Ottoman fleet. The day's observances include solemn Masses, processions, and the recitation of the Rosary, fostering a deep sense of communal prayer and gratitude. This annual celebration not only commemorates a historical victory but also reinforces the enduring belief in the protection and guidance of the Blessed Virgin Mary, reminding the faithful of her maternal presence in moments of peril and triumph. Marked by a mixture of solemnity and joy, the Feast of Our Lady of Victory continues to inspire and unite Catholics in a shared heritage of faith and fortitude.

Establishment of the Feast

The establishment of the Feast of Our Lady of Victory serves as a testament to the enduring conviction of faith and the recognition of divine intervention in human affairs. Stipulated by Pope Pius V, this liturgical celebration was first decreed on October 7, 1571, the very day of the Battle of Lepanto. The triumph of the Holy League, a coalition of Catholic maritime states, over the formidable Ottoman fleet was seen, by contemporaries and posterity alike, as nothing short of a miraculous deliverance.

Pope Pius V was a man imbued with an unshakeable zeal for the preservation and propagation of Christianity. A Dominican friar before ascending the Papal throne, his life was a testament to simplicity and piety. His decision to call for a feast day to honor Our Lady's intervention early testifies to his unwavering belief that the victory at Lepanto was won not merely by human strategy, but through divine grace. In announcing the establishment of this feast, the Pope underscored the vital role prayer had played in the Christian victory, particularly the Rosary, which he had fervently promoted among the faithful during the dark days leading to the battle.

The victory was attributed directly to the intercession of the Virgin Mary, as Pope Pius V had urged all of Christendom to pray the Holy Rosary for a successful outcome. While fleets clashed on the waters, countless prayers ascended to heaven. When it became clear that the Christian forces had triumphed, the Pope saw it as the unmistakable hand of Mary at work. Thus, the Feast of Our Lady of Victory was designed not only as a commemoration of a historic triumph but also as an enduring call to devotion.

The significance of establishing this feast goes beyond mere historical reminiscence; it served as a beacon of hope and faith during a time when Christendom faced existential threats from external forces. Aware of its broader spiritual implications, Pope Pius V intended that generations to come would remember the power of collective prayer and the ever-present guardianship of the Blessed Virgin. He envisioned a Europe united not only by political and military alliances but by a shared, unshakable faith.

The initial celebrations were marked by grand processions, vigil masses, and the recitation of the Rosary throughout the cities of Italy and beyond. Churches were adorned with special decorations, and elaborate liturgies were performed to give thanks for the victory granted through divine intercession. Over the years, these celebrations evolved and took various forms, influenced by local traditions and customs. Yet, the essence of the feast remained: a solemn yet jubilant acknowledgment of Mary's protective mantle over her people.

As the years progressed, the feast underwent minor transformations. In 1573, Pope Gregory XIII rebranded it as the Feast of the Holy Rosary, thus emphasizing the instrument through which divine favor was sought and obtained. This shift further ingrained the Rosary's significance in Catholic practice, making it an indispensable element of spiritual warfare. The connection to Our Lady of Victory was not lost but strengthened, as believers were continually reminded of the power encapsulated in the repetitive, meditative prayers of the Rosary.

Devotion to Our Lady of Victory became a fixture in the liturgical calendar, enduring through centuries of change and upheaval. Even during periods of internal struggle within the Church and the rise of secular ideologies that sought to diminish the role of religion in public life, the feast remained a unifying event. It prompted the faithful to reconnect with the spiritual heritage and to draw inspiration from the historical confluence of faith, courage, and divine assistance.

Furthermore, the establishment of this feast underscored the centrality of Marian devotion in Catholicism. It reminded the faithful of Mary's unique role as intercessor and protector. Through the feast, believers found solace and assurance that in moments of peril, one could always turn to the Blessed Virgin for aid. It was a celebration that fortified the communal and individual resolve to persevere in faith, regardless of the adversities faced.

Strategists and historians analyzing the feast's establishment might see a calculated move to bolster morale and unify divergent European forces under a common religious and cultural banner. In the volatile landscape of 16th-century Europe, where religious wars and political fracturing were commonplace, the Feast of Our Lady of Victory acted as a spiritual anchor. It fostered a collective identity rooted in shared faith and divine providence, elements critical to sustaining the momentum against persistent Ottoman threats.

Institutions and leaders within the Church also utilized this feast as a didactic tool. By linking military victory directly to intercessory prayer and divine will, they educated the laity about the potency of faith in action. This feast became an ecclesiastical instrument to teach the values of perseverance, piety, and communal solidarity. Through annual celebrations, homilies, and religious education, generations learned not only the history of the Battle of Lepanto but the indispensable role of spiritual discipline in achieving seemingly impossible victories.

One must also consider the artistic and cultural ramifications of establishing this feast. The Feast of Our Lady of Victory inspired an outpouring of devotional art, literature, and music, all created to honor Mary and commemorate the historic triumph. Churches commissioned paintings and sculptures depicting the battle and Mary's intervention, which served as both religious and educational artifacts. Hymns and liturgical music composed for the feast added another layer of cultural enrichment, offering the faithful an auditory experience of the divine moment they celebrated.

Though initially concentrated in Catholic Europe, the significance of the feast spread to various parts of the world through missionary efforts. Wherever the Church established itself, the Feast of Our Lady of Victory became part of the liturgical calendar, thus extending the narrative of divine intervention and Marian protection to new cultures and communities. This international reach not only preserved the memory of Lepanto but perpetuated the universal relevance of Marian devotion.

In modern times, the feast continues to be a pivotal event in the Church's liturgical life. Recent papacies have revisited and reinvigorated its celebration, using it as an occasion to call for global prayer and unity in the face of contemporary challenges. With the Church now more universally spread than ever, the Feast of Our Lady of Victory serves as a reminder that faith remains a constant, unifying force amid the vicissitudes of history.

The establishment of the Feast of Our Lady of Victory encapsulates a moment where heaven and earth seemingly intersected. Through its reverent observance, the faithful of today join with those of yesteryear in acknowledging the Providential hand that guides and sustains. The feast stands as an eternal witness to the Church's belief in the power of divine intervention, amplified through human cooperation in the form of prayer, and manifests in a spectacular historical narrative that continues to inspire and instruct.

By celebrating this feast, Catholics reaffirm their trust in Mary's intercession, drawing strength from a victory won centuries ago yet resonating with timeless significance. It is a feast rooted both in history and faith, inviting all to remember that in moments of peril, divine grace, accessed through earnest prayer, remains ever attainable.

Celebrations and Traditions

At the core of "The Feast of Our Lady of Victory" lies a tapestry of rich celebrations and time-honored traditions that testify to the enduring faith and gratitude of the Catholic Church. Established by Pope Pius V to commemorate the Christian victory at the Battle of Lepanto, this feast has since evolved to embody various forms of devotion, ceremonies, and cultural practices. Each October 7th, Catholics around the world unite to honor the Blessed Virgin Mary, acknowledging her intercession and the miraculous success attributed to the power of the Holy Rosary.

The festivities surrounding the Feast of Our Lady of Victory are as varied and intricate as the communities that observe them. In many towns and cities, elaborate processions are a highlight of the day. These processions often feature statues of the Virgin Mary, adorned with flowers and carried on the shoulders of the faithful. As the procession winds through the streets, participants chant hymns and pray the Rosary, their voices rising in a collective act of veneration. Such events serve to bring communities together, uniting them in a shared expression of faith and honor.

In coastal regions, particularly those with historical ties to maritime trade and exploration, the Feast of Our Lady of Victory takes on additional layers of significance. Here, boats decorated with garlands and icons of the Virgin Mary set out to sea in a ritualistic journey. Fishermen and sailors, mindful of their dependence on the blessings of the sea, pay homage to Our Lady, beseeching her protection and guidance. These maritime traditions underscore the battle's naval dimension and the Virgin's role as a celestial protector of those who traverse the waters.

Masses held on this feast day often mirror the solemnity and grandeur typically associated with major Catholic celebrations. Priests deliver homilies that recount the historical significance of the Battle of Lepanto and the intercessory power of the Holy Rosary. The liturgy is imbued with prayers, readings, and symbolic gestures that evoke the battle's narrative and the subsequent divine intervention. Among the most poignant moments is the communal recitation of the Rosary, involving congregants in a shared spiritual practice that links them directly to the events of 1571.

Besides these public festivities, many families observe the feast within the intimacy of their homes. It is not uncommon for households to create small altars dedicated to Our Lady of Victory, adorned with candles, rosaries, and images of the Virgin. Family members gather around these altars to pray, often including intentions for peace, protection, and thanksgiving. Such private devotions ensure that the feast's spiritual essence permeates daily life, fostering a sense of continuous connection with the divine.

Educational events also play a crucial role in the celebrations. Schools, particularly those with religious affiliations, seize the opportunity to impart the historical and spiritual lessons of Lepanto to their students. Through storytelling, reenactments, and art projects, children engage with the feast's themes and develop an appreciation for its significance. This educational component ensures that the legacy of the battle and the power of the Rosary are passed down to future generations, keeping the memory and reverence alive.

Gastronomy, too, finds its way into the feast's observance. Special dishes are prepared to honor Our Lady, with recipes often passed down through generations. These culinary traditions vary by region but commonly include foods symbolizing victory and abundance. Feasting together strengthens communal bonds and provides a tangible means of celebrating the Virgin Mary's intercession, making the day's spiritual joy manifest in a physical form.

The Feast of Our Lady of Victory is a liturgical celebration, but it also intersects with various cultural expressions. In some countries, the day coincides with national holidays or local festivities, blending religious observance with cultural identity. For instance, in Italy, where the feast originated, the day is marked by both religious and secular events, creating a multifaceted celebration that highlights the nation's historical devotion to the Virgin Mary.

Moreover, the feast has inspired artistic and creative expressions. Composers have written hymns and musical pieces to honor Our Lady of Victory, filling churches and homes with melodies that uplift the spirit. Artists contribute through paintings, sculptures, and other visual arts that capture the essence of the Battle of Lepanto and the subsequent divine intervention. These creative works serve as conduits for contemplation, allowing the faithful to engage with the feast's themes on a deeper, more personal level.

Ecumenical activities are also a noteworthy aspect of the feast's observance. Interfaith dialogues and joint prayer services bring together Christians of various denominations to celebrate the victory and acknowledge the shared Christian heritage. These events promote unity and mutual respect, reinforcing the idea that the triumph at Lepanto was a collective Christian victory, not limited to any single tradition or sect.

The Feast of Our Lady of Victory, in many ways, acts as a living bridge between past and present, connecting contemporary faithful with their historical predecessors. By engaging in these celebrations and traditions, Catholics reaffirm their devotion to the Virgin Mary and the Holy Rosary, while also perpetuating the memory of a pivotal moment in Christian history. The feast thus serves a dual purpose: it is both a commemoration of a miraculous victory and a testament to the enduring power of prayer and faith.

Indeed, the very essence of the feast lies in its capacity to bring together diverse expressions of faith, culture, and history into a unified celebration of divine intervention. Whether through grand public processions, intimate family prayers, educational programs, or artistic endeavors, the Feast of Our Lady of Victory continues to inspire and uplift, embodying a tradition that transcends time and place.

Chapter 12: The Aftermath of the Battle

The Battle of Lepanto, fought on October 7, 1571, left a profound mark on both the Ottoman Empire and Christian Europe. The immediate consequences for the Ottomans were devastating; the loss of a significant portion of their fleet and thousands of men dealt a severe blow to their naval dominance. On the Christian side, the victory was celebrated as a divine intervention, bolstering morale and strengthening the resolve of European powers to stand united against the Ottoman threat. This triumph went beyond military success, deeply influencing cultural and religious sentiments. The significance of the Holy Rosary, which many believed played a pivotal role in securing victory, was cemented in the collective consciousness, leading to widespread devotion. The impact of this battle resonated through the corridors of history, reshaping the geopolitical landscape and inspiring generations to perceive it as a clash not just of arms, but of civilizations and faiths.

Immediate Consequences for the Ottoman Empire

In the wake of the Battle of Lepanto, the Ottoman Empire faced a stark and immediate shift in its strategic and maritime capabilities. The defeat was a blow not only to its naval power but also to its expanding ambitions in the Mediterranean region. On October 7, 1571, the battle ceased, and so, too, did the Ottoman dream of an unchallenged dominance at sea.

The loss of a significant portion of their fleet had immediate ramifications. Ships that had once patrolled the waters as symbols of Ottoman might now lay ruined or captured by the forces of the Holy League. The destruction of at least 50 Ottoman galleys and the capture of approximately 120 more crippled their ability to project naval power. This level of loss was unprecedented and it dealt a severe blow to Ottoman maritime capacity. The immediate consequence of this was a restriction on their ability to reinforce and supply their outlying territories, especially those in North Africa and the Aegean Sea.

Moreover, the soldiers who perished were among the empire's most experienced mariners and fighters. The death of Ali Pasha, the commander of the Ottoman fleet, left a leadership vacuum that could not be immediately filled. This loss of seasoned commanders and troops further weakened the empire's military prowess. In the heart of the empire, the news of this defeat led to political turbulence. Sultan Selim II faced significant pressure from his advisors and the military elite, who demanded explanations for this unexpected loss. The defeat called into question the infallibility of Ottoman military strategy and leadership.

However, Ottoman resilience should not be underestimated. By the spring of the following year, efforts were already underway to rebuild the fleet. The Ottomans utilized their extensive resources and skilled shipbuilders to construct new vessels at an impressive pace. Nonetheless, the experience and expertise lost at Lepanto could not be so easily replaced. Although the empire managed to field a new navy relatively quickly, it took years before it could reclaim its former potency and confidence at sea.

Economically, the battle had a pressing impact. Naval construction demanded immense resources, and the empire had to divert funds from other projects to support the rebuilding effort. Trade routes, particularly those involving the transport of goods between the East and the West, were disrupted. This not only affected the Ottoman economy but also strained their relationships with various trading partners. Additionally, piracy along the Mediterranean, a constant bane to commerce, saw a temporary decrease in Ottoman control, leading to increased threats from corsairs and privateers.

Diplomatically, the defeat at Lepanto shattered the image of Ottoman invincibility that had been carefully cultivated over decades of conquests. European powers, who had previously felt the weight of Ottoman expansionist ambitions, saw an opportunity to challenge Ottoman supremacy. This shift in perception triggered several aggressive moves by European states, which now felt emboldened to press their advantage. Treaties previously weighted heavily in favor of Ottomans were re-examined and renegotiated, often at the expense of Ottoman strategic interests.

This loss also had a profound psychological impact within the empire. For a society that prided itself on its military supremacy, the Battle of Lepanto became a sobering reminder of their vulnerability. The sultan's court in Constantinople was rife with introspection and analysis, as military leaders sought to understand the failures and short-comings that led to such a catastrophic defeat. This loss eroded the morale of not only the navy but also the general populace, who had always viewed their military as the shield of Islam.

Religiously, the defeat was interpreted through various lenses. Some within the empire saw it as a divine displeasure, questioning whether the empire had strayed from its path of righteousness. This led to a renewed zeal in religious observance and a temporary surge in Islamic fundamentalism, as leaders and the populace alike sought to align themselves once more with their perception of divine will.

In contrast, the battle solidified the Holy League's belief in divine intervention, particularly through the intercession of the Virgin Mary and the power of the Rosary. The Christian victory was celebrated as an act of divine providence, a notion that further demoralized the Ottomans who grappled with the theological implications of their defeat. The notion that their defeat could be attributed to the grace of a Christian deity was unsettling and spurred a re-examination of religious and cultural narratives within the Ottoman lands.

Looking at the broader geopolitical landscape, the defeat at Lepanto had long-lasting repercussions. Although the Ottoman Empire would remain a formidable power for centuries, its westward expansion in Europe was effectively halted. This allowed the European powers, par-ticularly Spain and the Papal States, to consolidate and strengthen their defenses along the Mediterranean. It also allowed for a realignment of alliances and power structures that would shape European politics well into the future.

In conclusion, while the Ottoman Empire demonstrated remarkable resilience in the aftermath of Lepanto, the immediate consequences were profound and multifaceted. The destruction of their fleet, loss of seasoned leaders, economic strain, and the political and religious ramifications collectively marked a turning point. The empire, which had once seemed unstoppable, now had to navigate a new reality shaped by the shadows of a resounding defeat. The Battle of Lepanto was not just a clash of arms but a pivotal moment that reshaped the trajectory of one of history's greatest empires.

Impact on Christian Europe

The Battle of Lepanto marked a significant turning point for Christian Europe. It confirmed that the Ottoman Empire was not invincible. The victory brought a renewed sense of hope and confidence in Christian states that had long lived under the shadow of Ottoman expansion. The immediate impact on Christian Europe was manifold: the stop of Ottoman naval advancements in the Mediterranean, the bolstering of Christian morale, and a renewed unity among European Christian states.

The relief and euphoria that followed the news of Lepanto's victory were palpable throughout Europe. Churches rang their bells, and special masses were held in thanksgiving. The victory was seen as a divine endorsement of their cause. The prestige of the Pope, Saint Pius V, who had organized and inspired the Holy League, rose significantly. Many believed that the prayers he had fervently called for, especially through the Holy Rosary, had miraculously tilted the scales in favor of the Christian forces.

This victory fostered a renewed sense of purpose and unity among Christian powers, at least temporarily. Countries that had often found themselves at odds with one another—such as Spain and Venice—could put aside their differences, recognizing the greater threat posed by the Ottomans. The victory at Lepanto thus became a symbol of what could be achieved when Christian nations acted in unison toward a common goal.

The aftermath saw a rise in the popularity and devotion of the Holy Rosary. Recognizing the role that prayer was believed to have played, numerous devotions, confraternities, and chapels dedicated to the Rosary sprang up across Europe. The formation of these groups was not merely a religious reaction; it was a cultural shift that reinforced the collective Christian identity against the looming Islamic threat. The Holy Rosary became both a spiritual tool and a unifying symbol.

Culturally, the Battle of Lepanto resonated deeply within the Christian collective psyche. Artists, poets, and writers across Europe took inspiration from the event, immortalizing it in their works. The epic scope of the battle, combined with its perceived miraculous nature, provided fertile ground for a myriad of creative expressions. Paintings, epic poems, and songs celebrated the valor of the Christian fighters and the intercession of the Virgin Mary.

Politically, the victory did not lead to any immediate grand territorial gains for the Christian states, but it hindered the Ottoman naval dominance. Europe was no longer as vulnerable to maritime raids and invasions. This had a long-term stabilizing effect on the geopolitical landscape, allowing European nations to focus more on internal development and less on constant defensive posturing against the Turks.

However, the victory also imposed a brutal reality: it highlighted the continuing need for vigilance and unity among Christian states. The Ottoman Empire, though significantly weakened on the sea, remained a formidable force on land. This understanding led to an intermittent period of crusading efforts and defensive alliances, all nurtured by the echo of Lepanto's triumph. Future conflicts saw Christian armies mindful of the lessons learned from this naval engagement.

Theological reflection on the victory was profound. Many saw it as a concrete instance of divine intervention, an event where providence evidently favored the righteous path. The writings and sermons following the battle often highlighted the interplay between divine grace and human valor. Theologians and clerics drew from the victory morals and teachings about faith, perseverance, and the efficacy of collective prayer. These theological underpinnings would continue to echo through councils, synods, and religious literature.

In homes across Christian Europe, the stories of Lepanto became legendary. Parents told their children tales of gallant knights and miraculous turns of fate. The battle became a part of the collective memory, serving as a touchstone for Christian identity and valor. This cultural embedding reinforced societal values centered around courage, faith, and unity in the face of adversity.

All in all, the Battle of Lepanto and its aftermath had a profound and lasting impact on Christian Europe. It was not just a military victory; it was a spiritual and cultural watershed moment that redefined Christian Europe's approach to both external threats and internal unity. Churches embellished their altars with relics from the battle, art immortalized the heroism, and simple folk found renewed faith in their daily prayers. Lepanto became more than a battle; it became a beacon of what Christian Europe could achieve when united by faith and purpose.

Chapter 13: Long-Term Implications

The Battle of Lepanto, while a defining moment in its own right, catalyzed an evolution in naval warfare and recalibrated the balance of power within the European political sphere for centuries to come. The Christian victory not only curtailed the Ottoman naval dominance but also marked the ascendancy of more advanced European naval strategies and technologies. Nations realigned their priorities, forging alliances based on shared religious and political objectives, reaffirming the potency of a united Christendom against common foes. This seismic shift engendered a reverence for the Holy Rosary, symbolizing divine intervention, and fortified the cultural and spiritual fabric of Europe. The resulting geopolitical landscape experienced reverberations in trade, military organization, and diplomatic relations that would sculpt the trajectory of Western civilization well beyond the Renaissance. By reevaluating these enduring legacies, historians and strategists discern how this singular event encapsulates the intersection of faith, power, and the relentless tide of progress.

Changes in Naval Warfare

The Battle of Lepanto on October 7, 1571, marked a transformative period in naval warfare, creating ripples that would influence maritime strategy for centuries. Prior to Lepanto, naval engagements primarily involved galley ships propelled by oarsmen, an inheritance from classical antiquity. These vessels, though agile and instrumental in coastal assaults, were limited in their range and firepower. The Christian coalition at Lepanto, however, subtly but significantly altered these conventions—not merely by the types of ships deployed but by the tactical doctrines they embraced.

One of the most striking changes after Lepanto was the increased reliance on gunpowder artillery. Although cannons had been used in naval battles before, the Christian fleet's effective deployment of onboard artillery at Lepanto underscored their potential. Galleasses, heavily armed ships positioned at both ends of the Christian line, created destructive volleys that shattered the Ottoman formations. Their effective use of broadside cannons prefigured the future dominance of ship-mounted artillery over traditional boarding tactics.

In addition to changes in armament, the tactics used at Lepanto heralded a shift towards more sophisticated coordination and strategy during naval engagements. The Holy League's ability to unify under a single command, led by Don Juan of Austria, showcased the value of coordinated, hierarchical leadership in achieving strategic objectives. The Christian fleet's compact crescent formation facilitated efficient communication and mutual support, drastically reducing the likelihood of isolated ships being overwhelmed by the Ottoman forces.

Moreover, Lepanto demonstrated the strategic importance of intelligence and reconnaissance. The Christian fleet benefited from superior information about Ottoman movements, which was crucial in their decision to confront the Ottoman fleet in the Gulf of Patras. This focus on gathering and acting on reliable intelligence would become a hallmark of naval strategy in subsequent centuries, influencing the development of dedicated reconnaissance ships and later, submarine warfare.

The Battle of Lepanto was not merely a contest of brute force but a testament to advances in naval architecture and design. The development and deployment of the galleass, a hybrid between a galley and a sailing ship, underscored an evolving understanding of naval versatility. These ships, featuring both oars and sails, combined the maneuverability of traditional galleys with the firepower of larger sailing vessels. Their success at Lepanto accelerated the decline of the oar-powered galley and spurred innovations in ship design, leading towards the dominance of sailing warships.

Another noteworthy aspect brought to the forefront by Lepanto was the vital role of morale and spiritual solidarity in wartime efforts. The Christian forces' unity was profoundly shaped by their shared faith and the invocation of the Holy Rosary, believed to have brought divine favor. This spiritual dimension bolstered the resolve and combat effectiveness of the Holy League's sailors, demonstrating that the psychological and inspirational aspects of warfare were as crucial as the physical ones.

Lepanto also precipitated an evolution in crew composition and training. The Christian fleet's emphasis on training and discipline contrasted sharply with the often coerced and enslaved Ottoman rowers. This highlighted the efficacy of having a professional, motivated naval workforce, an approach that would eventually lead to the establishment of formal naval academies and standing navies in European powers.

Navigational techniques witnessed refinement in the battle's wake as well. The success at Lepanto underscored the importance of mastering the maritime environment. Subsequent naval powers invested heavily in cartography, the development of more precise maritime compasses, and advancements in celestial navigation. These innovations extended the operational range of naval forces, opening new theaters of conflict and opportunities for exploration.

The ripple effects of Lepanto's shifts extended to geopolitical dynamics, further shaping naval warfare. The battle proved that coordinated Christian naval coalitions could successfully counter Ottoman expansionist ambitions in the Mediterranean. This realization encouraged European powers to forge alliances and implement collaborative maritime defense strategies, a pragmatic approach that would find echoes in later coalitions and alliances during global conflicts, such as the World Wars.

Furthermore, Lepanto underscored the strategic importance of maintaining control over key maritime chokepoints. The Holy League's victory ensured Christian dominance over the crucial naval routes in the Mediterranean, stymying Ottoman attempts to disrupt Christian trade and supply lines. This awareness influenced the subsequent European colonial and trading empires to secure and fortify important maritime passages around the globe, such as the Strait of Gibraltar, the Suez Canal, and the Cape of Good Hope.

As the notion of national navies began to take form, the influence of Lepanto reverberated through naval doctrines and treatises, contributing to the development of modern naval theory. Theologians, strategists, and historians alike scrutinized the battle's details, drawing lessons that informed the evolution of naval strategy. These analyses helped refine the principles of sea power, encouraging naval powers to adopt strategies that emphasized flexibility, combined arms, and the operational integration of diverse naval assets.

Interestingly, the aftermath of Lepanto also heralded advancements in naval logistics and supply chain management. The ability to sustain a fleet over extended campaigns by ensuring a steady supply of provisions, armaments, and reinforcements became a focal point of naval strategy. This logistical acumen was vital for maintaining prolonged naval superiority, influencing subsequent maritime campaigns and the establishment of overseas naval bases.

In summary, the Battle of Lepanto represented a watershed moment in naval warfare, signaling the transition from medieval maritime practices to early modern naval doctrines. The battle emphasized the growing importance of artillery, complex ship designs, and specialized training. It also highlighted the strategic significance of intelligence, morale, and logistics. As a confluence of tactical innovation, strategic foresight, and spiritual unity, Lepanto's impact on naval warfare cannot be overstated. The lessons derived from this naval engagement would go on to shape the course of naval history, leaving an indelible mark on Christian Europe's martial and spiritual landscape.

Influence on European Political Landscape

The Battle of Lepanto, fought on October 7, 1571, was not merely a naval skirmish; it was a pivotal moment that reshaped the European political landscape. The Holy League's victory over the Ottoman Empire had profound implications, which reverberated throughout the continent, fundamentally altering the course of European history. This section delves into the multifaceted ways in which Lepanto influenced the political dynamics across Europe.

An immediate consequence of the Holy League's triumph was the bolstering of confidence among Christian European powers. The Ottomans' seeming invincibility was shattered, and for the first time in decades, European nations felt a renewed sense of security. This shift in confidence emboldened various European states to engage more aggressively in their political and military interests, knowing they could stand against the might of the Ottoman Empire.

The victory also played a significant role in shaping the alliances and rivalries within Europe. The Holy League, composed primarily of the Papal States, Spain, Venice, Genoa, and other smaller entities, showcased the power of a unified Christian front. However, the alliances were not without internal strife and competition. Spain and Venice, two principal members of the League, often had conflicting interests that simmered below the surface. The aftermath of the battle saw these tensions occasionally flare up, influencing their political maneuvers for decades to come.

A particularly striking development was the strengthening of the Papal influence. Pope Pius V, a tireless advocate for the Holy League, emerged as a central figure in European politics. The victory at Lepanto reinforced the Papacy's spiritual and temporal authority, making it a formidable force in political decisions. This enhanced influence allowed the Papacy to play a more significant role in mediating conflicts and shaping the geopolitical landscape.

The battle also contributed to the decline of Ottoman influence in the Mediterranean, marking the beginning of the end for Ottoman expansion into Europe. This decline altered the strategic priorities of European nations. Countries such as Spain and Austria shifted their focus from purely defensive postures against the Ottomans to more expansive endeavors, including the Spanish colonization efforts in the New World and Austria's influence in the Balkans.

Moreover, the victory at Lepanto had far-reaching effects on trade routes and economic power structures. With the Ottoman threat diminished, European maritime routes were safer, leading to an increase in trade and commerce. The rising economic fortunes of states such as Venice and Genoa facilitated the prosperity of their merchant classes, which in turn had political ramifications. Wealthier states had more resources to invest in military technology and infrastructure, thereby reinforcing their political power.

The ideological ramifications of the battle were equally significant. Lepanto was framed as a divine victory for Christianity over Islam, reinforcing religious zeal and justifying the political ambitions of European powers under the guise of a Christian mission. This ideological framing maintained its influence well beyond the immediate aftermath of the battle, affecting European politics deeply. It provided the moral justification for future conflicts and crusades, which were often cloaked in religious rhetoric.

In the broader tapestry of European history, the Battle of Lepanto also served as a unifying mythos that rallied disparate states under the banner of a common cause. While political fragmentation continued to characterize much of Europe, the memory of Lepanto—symbolizing unity against a common threat—remained a powerful narrative. This narrative was exploited by rulers and statesmen to foster nationalistic and religious fervor that would be harnessed in various political agendas throughout the succeeding centuries.

Furthermore, the impact of Lepanto was felt in the political landscape of individual states. For instance, Spain, under King Philip II, capitalized on the victory to consolidate its dominance in Europe. The victory at Lepanto provided Philip II with the prestige and moral authority to pursue his ambitions more aggressively, including the eventual launch of the Spanish Armada against England. Although the Armada's fate was less fortunate, the confidence imbued by Lepanto's victory lingered in Spanish political and military strategies.

Venice, an indispensable partner in the Holy League, experienced a complex political aftershock. While the victory temporarily alleviated the Ottoman pressure, Venice's intricate and often tenuous diplomatic relations with both its European allies and the Ottomans required skillful navigation. The political landscape for Venice was one of cautious expansion and diplomacy, balancing between asserting its influence and maintaining its crucial commercial ties.

The influence of the Battle of Lepanto on the European political landscape also reached beyond the Mediterranean. Nations that were not directly involved in the conflict, such as France and England, observed the unfolding events with keen interest. The battle's outcome influenced their foreign policies and military strategies, as they adjusted to a geopolitical environment where the Ottoman threat had been significantly checked. The recalibration of foreign policies led to shifting alliances and new power dynamics within Europe, as states sought to capitalize on the altered political landscape.

The influence on the political landscape extended into the cultural and intellectual realms. The Renaissance, already flourishing in Europe, was given an additional impetus by the outcome of Lepanto. The victory was celebrated in art, literature, and music, contributing to the cultural identity of Europe and reinforcing the notion of a resurgent Christendom. This cultural celebration had political undertones, as rulers and states leveraged the victory's symbolism to legitimize their power and inspire their subjects.

Moreover, the victory at Lepanto played a crucial role in the development of Western naval warfare. It demonstrated the effectiveness of galley fleets and the tactical importance of coordinated naval strategies. European powers drew lessons from the battle that informed their naval policies and technological advancements, which in turn affected their political and military strategies. The legacy of Lepanto was visible in the evolving naval doctrines of the time, influencing the balance of power on the seas and subsequently the geopolitical landscape of Europe.

In conclusion, the Battle of Lepanto had a profound and multifaceted influence on the European political landscape. It reshaped alliances, bolstered confidence among Christian nations, and shifted the focus of political and military strategies. The Papal authority was reinforced, and the decline of Ottoman influence allowed for new economic opportunities and strategic priorities. The ideological and cultural ramifications further cemented the battle's legacy, creating a powerful narrative that continued to influence European politics for generations. It is within this intricate web of political, cultural, and ideological shifts that the true significance of Lepanto can be understood, marking it as a defining moment in European history.

Chapter 14: The Battle of Lepanto in Art and Literature

The Battle of Lepanto, a pivotal and heroic struggle, has resonated through the annals of time, immortalized in both art and literature. From the vivid canvases of Titian and Veronese to the stirring verses of G.K. Chesterton's epic poem "Lepanto," creatives have sought to capture the grandeur and divine significance of this momentous event. The battle's depiction serves not merely as a historical recounting but as a narrative of faith triumphing over adversity, reflecting the collective memory and spiritual valor of Christendom. These artistic and literary works contribute to a shared cultural heritage, ensuring that the heroism displayed and the divine intercession believed to have turned the tide at Lepanto are forever remembered. Through these mediums, the Battle of Lepanto lives on, not simply as a chapter in history, but as an enduring symbol of the enduring struggle between faith and conquest, unity and division. The legacy of this clash on October 7, 1571, continues to inspire and elevate the human spirit, cementing the battle's place within the hallowed halls of both historical and sacred narratives.

Contemporary Accounts and Depictions

In the immediate aftermath of the Battle of Lepanto, poets, historians, and artists from across Europe became swift chroniclers of this momentous event, capturing its significance through their respective mediums. Their creative responses served not just as reflections but also as instruments of commemoration and propagation of the Christian victory over the Ottoman forces. The battle, fought on October 7, 1571, reverberated through the cultural consciousness of the time, leaving an indelible mark on art and literature that has persisted for centuries.

One of the earliest and most influential accounts came from the pen of the Spanish poet Fernando de Herrera. His epic poem, "La Guerra de Lepanto," lionized Don Juan of Austria, the commander of the Holy League fleet, elevating him to an almost mythic stature. Through rhythmic verses and vivid imagery, Herrera immortalized the clash of galleys, the crash of swords, and the victorious ascent of the Christian standard upon the captured Ottoman flagship. Herrera's work permeated the collective psyche, serving as a literary beacon that celebrated both the military prowess and divine favor that secured the victory.

Likewise, the Italian writer Gianfrancesco Albani crafted meticulous prose accounts detailing the battlefield's intricacies. Albani's chronicles were renowned for their accuracy and vivid portrayal of the strategic maneuvers and pivotal moments of the engagement. His works provided a factual narrative that complemented the more stylized and poetic renditions, lending a credibility and depth to the historical record. Through Albani's descriptions, readers could almost hear the cacophony of battle and feel the tension of those decisive hours.

These contemporary literary works were not confined to land-locked narratives; they seeped into the letters and reports of sailors and commanders who partook in the battle. Personal correspondences often revealed a blend of stark reality and subtle heroism, painting pictures of both valor and vulnerability. For instance, the detailed letters from naval officers to their sovereigns and families illuminated the harrowing experiences aboard the galleys, the fervent prayers uttered in the heat of battle, and the enduring faith that victory seemed to vindicate.

Art, too, became a powerful medium of remembrance and interpretation. Iconographic representations of the Battle of Lepanto appeared prominently in churches, palaces, and public spaces throughout Catholic Europe. One of the most celebrated examples is the painting by Paolo Veronese, completed in 1572, which resides in the Doge's Palace in Venice. Veronese's canvas captures the grandeur and tumult of the naval clash, with vibrant hues and dynamic compositions reflecting the intense drama and spiritual significance of the event. The artwork conveys not merely a historical episode but an epic tableau where divine intervention and human endeavor intersect.

Another notable contemporary depiction is found in the work of Titian, whose allegorical implication of the battle in his painting "The Allegory of the Battle of Lepanto" merges human figures and celestial beings, imbuing the scene with a profound theological narrative. Titian's art served not just as a historical record but as a theological commentary, stressing the belief in the intercession of the Virgin Mary and the power of the Holy Rosary, which many contemporaries attributed as pivotal to the victory.

The engravings of the period, such as those by Martino Rota, offered another dimension of documentation. These engravings provided detailed and accessible imagery that could be widely reproduced, ensuring that the memory of Lepanto reached even the modest households far removed from the centers of political power. Rota's work elucidated the geographical layout of the battle, the arrangement of the fleets, and key moments of engagement, becoming essential educational tools in both secular and religious contexts.

Moreover, the dramatic representations of the battle spread to the theater. Playwrights like Lope de Vega in Spain dramatized the heroics of Don Juan and the Holy League, weaving together history, politics, and theology in performances that captivated audiences. These plays were not only entertainment but potent vehicular for propagating a sense of shared identity and triumph among the European populace.

The influence of the Battle of Lepanto on contemporary accounts and depictions also resonated through the sermons and homiletic literature of the time. Preachers across Europe took to their pulpits to extol the battle as a divine endorsement of Christian unity and perseverance. Sermons of the era frequently drew upon the imagery of Lepanto to illustrate the virtues of courage, faith, and divine providence, reinforcing the cultural and spiritual significance of the event.

In addition to literary and artistic interpretations, the music of the period also reverberated with the echoes of Lepanto. Composers like Andrea Gabrieli crafted motets and orchestral pieces that celebrated the victory. The musical compositions often incorporated liturgical themes, intertwining the historical victory with the spiritual narrative, thus reinforcing the perception of Lepanto as a manifestation of divine will.

Venetian mosaics, such as those adorning the walls of the Basilica di San Marco, also played a role in preserving and celebrating the memory of the battle. These intricate artworks blended artistic skill with theological symbolism, depicting not just the physical acts of war but the celestial battles between good and evil. The mosaics symbolized a united Christendom under divine protection, with the figure of the Virgin Mary often depicted as overseeing the battle, further cementing her role as a spiritual intercessor.

Theological writings of the time were not immune to the influence of Lepanto. The battle served as a case study for theologians who were keen to interpret contemporary events through a spiritual lens. Treatises from scholars such as Cardinal Guglielmo Sirleto argued that Lepanto was a manifest sign of divine favor, using the event to advocate for the power and necessity of the Rosary in both personal and communal piety. These writings had a lasting impact, reinforcing theological doctrines that would endure long after the battle itself had faded from living memory.

Institutions like the Jesuit colleges also contributed to the proliferation of Lepanto's memory through their educational curriculum. Jesuit scholars integrated accounts of the battle into their teachings, emphasizing the interplay between divine providence and human agency in historical events. This integration ensured that future generations of leaders, both clerical and lay, would appreciate the historical and religious significance of Lepanto, perpetuating its legacy within the Catholic intellectual tradition.

In summary, the contemporary accounts and depictions of the Battle of Lepanto formed a rich tapestry that wove together art, literature, theology, and personal narratives. They served to memorialize a pivotal moment in history, reinforcing the themes of divine intervention and the resilience of faith. These works not only documented the past but also shaped the cultural and religious identity of Europe for centuries to come, underscoring the battle as a seminal event in the collective memory of Christendom.

Legacy in Modern Culture

The legacy of the Battle of Lepanto extends far beyond the annals of history; it reverberates through modern culture in ways both subtle and profound. The battle's depiction in art and literature has continued to inspire and shape the imaginations of artists, writers, and thinkers. One could argue that its significance has only grown with time as each generation reinterprets and reimagines its story to suit the cultural and ideological context of the age.

In the realm of visual art, the Battle of Lepanto has been memorialized in myriad ways—from grandiose oil paintings in the Baroque period to contemporary installations that interpret the clash through a more abstract lens. Yet, what's consistent is the sense of epic struggle and divine intervention that these works convey. The intricate tapestries and frescoes on display in various European cathedrals and museums highlight not only the fierce combat but also the celestial endorsement that many believe was pivotal in the Christian fleet's victory.

The power of the battle's imagery finds a strong foothold in literature as well. Renowned poets and authors, such as Miguel de Cervantes —who himself fought in the battle—have rendered it in evocative prose and verse. Cervantes' portrayal imbues the event with a sense of epic grandeur, embedding it deeply within the cultural psyche of Spain and, by extension, the wider world.

Fast forward to the modern era, and the legacy of Lepanto continues to be fertile ground for creative exploration. Contemporary novels and films often revisit the battle, each bringing a new perspective—sometimes questioning old narratives, sometimes reaffirming them. The battle's setting and characters provide a rich tableau for storytelling, allowing modern audiences to wrestle with issues of faith, courage, and unity just as their ancestors did.

Modern digital media have also embraced the Battle of Lepanto. Video games, for instance, offer interactive experiences where players can engage directly with this historical event, making strategic decisions that echo those faced by the Christian commanders. These games add a layer of personal connection to the historical narrative, letting players relive the complexities and stakes of the battle.

Beyond the traditional arts, the legacy of Lepanto finds resonance in the intellectual and spiritual life of today. Seminaries and universities often include the study of the battle in courses dealing with European history, military strategy, and religious studies. These academic pursuits do more than just recount a historical event; they explore its theological and philosophical ramifications. The idea of divine intervention, embodied by the passing of the Holy Rosary among the fleet's sailors, finds new interpretations in these scholarly circles.

Public commemorations and reenactments also play a part, keeping the memory of Lepanto alive within communities. These events serve not only as educational tools but also as touchstones of cultural identity, particularly for Roman Catholics. The annual Feast of Our Lady of Victory, celebrated on October 7, sees parishes worldwide reflecting on the importance of the battle, with processions, masses, and recitals that underline the ongoing relevance of this historic victory.

The influence of the Battle of Lepanto extends to the realms of modern political and military thought as well. Strategists and historians often cite the battle when discussing the evolution of naval tactics and the importance of alliance-building. The concept of a united front against a common foe, as demonstrated by the Holy League, serves as a case study in coalition warfare, relevant even in today's geopolitical landscape. The blending of faith and strategy that characterized the Christian armada offers unique insights into how ideological and military objectives can align and sometimes conflict.

Moreover, the enduring legacy of Lepanto in modern culture highlights the intersection of history, religion, and myth. While the battle was undoubtedly a significant military engagement, its portrayal often elevates it into the realm of legend. This mythic dimension can serve various purposes: it can be a source of nationalistic pride, a call to religious devotion, or a cautionary tale about the costs of conflict. It's this versatile legacy that allows the Battle of Lepanto to remain a compelling subject for modern audiences.

To appreciate the full impact of Lepanto on modern culture, one must consider the symbiotic relationship between historical events and their subsequent interpretations. The battle's significance wasn't solely cemented by the victory itself but by the myriad ways it has been remembered, retold, and re-envisioned. Every artistic depiction, literary work, or scholarly treatise adds another layer to the rich tapestry of Lepanto's legacy.

In conclusion, the Battle of Lepanto occupies a unique space in modern culture. Its legacy is not confined to the pages of history books but lives on in the art, literature, and collective memory of societies across the world. From dramatic canvases to thought-provoking novels and dynamic digital media, the story of this momentous battle continues to captivate and inspire, affirming its enduring relevance through the ages.

Chapter 15: The Battle's Significance in World History

The Battle of Lepanto, fought on October 7, 1571, was not just a pivotal moment in the annals of Christian and Ottoman conflicts but a turning point with far-reaching implications in world history. This clash halted the westward advance of the Ottoman Empire, preserving the Christian dominion over European seas and proving that the seemingly insurmountable tide of Ottoman conquest could indeed be challenged. Strategically, it underscored the importance of naval power and collaboration among disparate Christian kingdoms, weaving a tapestry of political and military alliances that would influence European geopolitics for centuries. For historians, Lepanto stands as a testament to the resilience and resolve of a united Christendom, reshaping the balance of power in the Mediterranean and heralding a new era in naval warfare. This epic encounter, thus, not only secured immediate victories but also furnished enduring lessons on the potentials and perils of unity against a formidable foe, offering invaluable insights for strategists and scholars alike.

Historical Reevaluation

As time marches forward, the significance of historical events often undergoes reevaluation. The Battle of Lepanto, long heralded as a Christian triumph over the advancing forces of the Ottoman Empire, invites such scrutiny. The reevaluation of this pivotal event uncovers layers of complexity and varying perspectives that enrich our understanding of its role in world history.

The Battle of Lepanto was fought on October 7, 1571, marking a watershed moment in the conflict between the Christian maritime powers of Europe and the formidable Ottoman Navy. For centuries, historians and theologians alike viewed this victory as a divine favor, a miraculous intervention credited to the intercession of the Holy Rosary and the Blessed Virgin Mary. Through a modern lens, however, more pragmatic interpretations have emerged, offering critical insights into the strategic, political, and cultural ramifications of the battle.

Examining the battle through the strategic objectives of both coalitions reveals a chessboard of geopolitical maneuvers. The Holy League, formed under the auspices of Pope Pius V, comprised a diverse but unified Christian alliance. The victory at Lepanto thwarted the Ottoman's ambitions to dominate the Mediterranean Sea, shifting the balance of power in favor of Europe. This perspective underscores the importance of coalition warfare and diplomacy. The Ottomans, conversely, had to reassess their maritime strategies, prompting changes that would affect future engagements.

The reevaluation process doesn't stop at strategy. Modern historians delve into the socio-political contexts that framed the battle. The Christian victory at Lepanto wasn't just a triumph of naval prowess; it symbolized the resilience of European Christendom at a time when the Ottoman Empire seemed unstoppable. This bolstered the morale of Christian Europe, reinforcing a collective identity rooted in a shared religious and cultural heritage. The victory also solidified the Pope's influence, reaffirming the spiritual unity of diverse European states under a common Christian cause.

It's also imperative to recontextualize the significance of the Battle of Lepanto in the wider narrative of Ottoman-European relations. While the battle thwarted immediate Ottoman expansions, it did not spell the end of Ottoman influence. The empire remained a dominant force, and its legacy continued to shape Mediterranean geopolitics. Understanding this dynamic offers insights into the resilience and adaptability of both the Ottoman Empire and European states, highlighting a nuanced balance of power rather than an absolute victory or defeat.

Cultural reevaluation brings to light the profound impact of the Battle of Lepanto on the arts and collective memory. The epic accounts, paintings, and literature that immortalized the event often emphasize the heroism and divine providence attributed to the Christian forces. Yet, contemporary analyses suggest that these depictions served more than an artistic purpose; they were also tools of propaganda that reinforced the victorious narrative. Thus, reevaluating these cultural artifacts provides a window into how societies construct and perpetuate historical memory.

Turning our attention to the theological interpretations, the reevaluation does not diminish the role of faith but rather places it within a broader historical framework. The Holy Rosary and the intercession of the Virgin Mary remain central to the narrative for many believers. Modern theological discourse, however, encourages a deeper understanding of how such events galvanize faith communities, inspiring subsequent generations to draw strength from these traditions. The Battle of Lepanto serves as a testament to the enduring power of faith in shaping historical and cultural landscapes.

In assessing the lessons of the Battle of Lepanto for modern times, today's strategists and historians discern parallels with contemporary conflicts. The importance of coalition-building, the influence of technology on warfare, and the role of leadership in critical moments are themes that resonate through the ages. As such, the Battle of Lepanto is not merely a historical artifact but a case study in the complexities of conflict and cooperation, bearing relevance to current geopolitical strategies and military doctrines.

Furthermore, reevaluation accommodates the perspectives of those who were on the losing side. Ottoman records and narratives provide valuable insights into how the battle was perceived and its repercussions managed within the empire. This includes shifts in naval tactics, political realignments, and internal reflections on the causes of their defeat. Such perspectives enrich the historical dialogue, fostering a more balanced and comprehensive understanding.

As historiography evolves, the reevaluation of key events like the Battle of Lepanto becomes indispensable for a fuller appraisal of their significance. It is through this continuous process of reassessment that history retains its dynamism, allowing each generation to draw meaningful connections between the past and the present. The Battle of Lepanto, while a moment of glory in the annals of Christian Europe, reveals itself as a multifaceted episode, rich with lessons that transcend its immediate aftermath.

This holistic approach to reevaluation highlights the interconnectedness of historical forces, the interplay of divine and human actions, and the enduring quest for meaning in the unfolding tapestry of world events. Whether viewed through the lenses of strategy, politics, culture, or theology, the Battle of Lepanto stands as a monumental example of how triumph and tribulation are interwoven in the grand narrative of history.

Lessons for Modern Times

The Battle of Lepanto, a monumental clash between Christian Europe and the advancing Ottoman Empire, still reverberates through the historical, strategic, and theological landscapes of the modern world. The battle, held on October 7, 1571, marked not just a military triumph but an enduring emblem of strategic unity and religious zeal. As we dissect its lessons for our contemporary context, one must appreciate the multi-faceted dimensions—from strategic alliances to the moral convictions that fortified them.

First, the enduring lesson of unity cannot be overstated. In an age where fragmentation and division seem omnipresent across societal, political, and even religious domains, the Battle of Lepanto serves as a salient reminder of the potency of coalition building. The Holy League, under the auspices of Pope Pius V, showcased an unprecedented unification of disparate European powers. These nations set aside their parochial conflicts in favor of a collective, existential defense. Modern strategists, whether in geopolitical realms or corporate arenas, would do well to study this paradigm of unity. Diverse entities, when aligned by a common purpose, can surmount otherwise insurmountable challenges.

Conversely, the battle underscores the disastrous consequences of overreach and hubris. The Ottoman Empire, expanding relentlessly, met a formidable resistance they perhaps underestimated. This is a timeless cautionary tale against overestimating one's reach and underestimating an opponent's resolve. Businesses, political entities, and even defense organizations today must recognize the importance of strategic humility. Flexibility and an accurate assessment of one's limitations and the adversary's strengths are crucial for long-term success.

In parallel, the Battle of Lepanto highlighted the critical role of leadership. Don Juan of Austria, a young and relatively inexperienced commander, rose to the occasion, embodying both tactical acumen and inspirational leadership. Modern leaders should draw inspiration from Don Juan's ability to galvanize a coalition through vision, courage, and decisiveness. Effective leadership is not merely about strategy but also about inspiring and instilling confidence. When people are driven by a steadfast belief in their leader's vision, they can achieve what may seem impossible.

Moreover, the battle underscores the importance of technological adaptation. In this naval confrontation, the Christian forces innovated with the galeasse, a heavily armed and maneuverable warship that played a pivotal role in their victory. The willingness to adapt and incorporate new technologies can be decisive. Contemporary militaries, businesses, and governments must prioritize innovation, continuously adapting their strategies to incorporate technological advancements. In a rapidly evolving world, stagnation can be as dangerous as outright defeat.

Another profound takeaway lies in the power of moral and spiritual dimensions. The invocation of the Holy Rosary and the sense of divine support galvanized the Christian forces in a way that transcended mere military might. This spiritual morale, fueled by a collective sense of divine purpose, was indispensable. In our modern, often secular world, the power of a shared moral or ethical vision should not be underestimated. Whether in social movements, organizational culture, or national endeavors, the alignment of actions with deeply held beliefs can inspire unparalleled commitment and perseverance.

A lesson closely tied to this spiritual dimension is the concept of resilience through faith. The aftermath of the Battle of Lepanto saw a renewed vigor in Christian Europe, a sense of divine vindication that bolstered morale and unity. Today, resilience—whether in personal, organizational, or national contexts—often finds its roots in a deeper sense of purpose. Faith-based resilience can be profoundly potent, nurturing a belief that challenges can be overcome by adhering to one's core values and beliefs.

The Battle of Lepanto also provides valuable insights into the importance of intelligence and prior knowledge. The effective use of reconnaissance and the understanding of Ottoman strategies allowed the Holy League to anticipate and counteract their moves. In an age where information is power, this lesson resonates strongly. Modern strategic planning must prioritize intelligence, not just in military contexts but across all domains where understanding the landscape—whether it be market conditions or geopolitical tensions—can profoundly affect outcomes.

The battle's legacy is not just cemented in historical annals but also preserved in cultural and artistic expressions. From literature to visual arts, the valor and drama of Lepanto have been immortalized. This highlights the importance of cultural memory in sustaining the ethos of a society. Modern societies should recognize the vitality of preserving and honoring significant historical events. This not only fosters a sense of identity and continuity but also provides a reservoir of lessons and inspirations for future challenges.

Equally significant is the lesson of strategic foresight. The Christian powers, under the visionary guidance of Pope Pius V, recognized the necessity of preemptive action. By taking the battle to the Mediterranean, they strategically forestalled a possible Ottoman expansion into Europe. Today's leaders must similarly exercise foresight, anticipating potential challenges and addressing them proactively. Complacency is often the precursor to crises; foresight is its antidote.

At the organizational level, Lepanto's teaching lies in the value of well-coordinated logistics and supply chains. The Holy League's ability to assemble, equip, and sustain a massive fleet was a logistical triumph. Modern enterprises, particularly those managing large-scale operations, can derive valuable lessons from this. Effective logistics and supply chain management can be the backbone of successful operations, enabling agility and resilience in the face of disruptions.

Lastly, the intrinsic value of commemoration and tradition offers vital lessons. The establishment of the Feast of Our Lady of Victory commemorates not just a military triumph but a decisive moment of unity and faith. Traditions and commemorations serve as cultural anchors, reminding societies of their foundational values and shared histories. In a rapidly changing world, these anchors provide stability and a sense of continuity, reinforcing collective identity and purpose.

In synthesizing the lessons of Lepanto, it becomes clear that this historic battle transcends its temporal confines, offering timeless wisdom applicable to contemporary challenges. Unity, leadership, technological innovation, moral conviction, foresight, and strategic adaptability form a corpus of lessons that resonate across centuries. The Battle of Lepanto, with its rich tapestry of historical, strategic, and spiritual dimensions, remains a beacon, illuminating pathways for modern times.

In conclusion, as we reflect on the significance of Lepanto in world history, we must not merely recount its events but embody its lessons. The confluence of strategic foresight, unyielding faith, and cohesive effort manifested in this battle offers enduring guidance. Whether confronting geopolitical challenges, organizational hurdles, or societal shifts, the Battle of Lepanto remains a profound teacher, guiding us towards a more unified, resilient, and visionary future.

Conclusion

The intertwining narratives of the Holy House of Loreto, the Holy Rosary, and the Battle of Lepanto are more than mere historical episodes—they form a divine tapestry revealing how faith and courage can redefine the course of history. The significance of these events extends beyond their temporal context, echoing through the corridors of time and imparting lessons that continue to resonate.

The Holy House of Loreto, with its miraculous journey from Nazareth to Italy, stands as a symbol of divine providence. It embodies the belief that God's intervention is not confined to the realms of the spiritual but manifests palpably in the material world. This venerated house, revered for its sacred association with the Virgin Mary, also served as a beacon of hope and unity for the Christian forces at Lepanto. It is a living testament to the faith's sustaining power, especially in times of turmoil and uncertainty.

In parallel, the Holy Rosary, integral to the faithful's spiritual arsenal, emerges as a testament to the power of prayer. It is not merely a sequence of recitations; it is a meditative journey into the mysteries of Christ, fostering a deep, personal connection with the divine. The Rosary's role in the Battle of Lepanto cannot be overstated. As soldiers and sailors clutched their Rosaries, intertwining their prayers with their actions, they underscored the belief that spiritual warfare is as real and significant as the physical battles they faced.

The Battle of Lepanto itself, dramatic and decisive, marked a pivotal moment in the clash of civilizations between Christian Europe and the Ottoman Empire. It was a battle not just of navies but of wills, strategies, and, ultimately, faiths. The strategic brilliance exhibited by the commanders and the relentless courage of the warriors refocused the direction of European history. Lepanto proved that unity and faith could indeed turn the tide against seemingly insurmountable odds, altering the geopolitical landscape of its time.

Saint Pius V, with his unwavering faith and decisive leadership, emerges as a central figure who galvanized the Christian forces. His life and papacy reflect the profound influence that a single, faith-driven individual can exert on history. Through his call for the Holy League and the initiation of a vast spiritual campaign, he encapsulated the Church's role not merely as a spiritual entity but as an active participant in shaping world events.

In examining the Holy League's formation and the subsequent battle, we unravel the intricate web of alliances and strategies that underpinned this historic event. The coalition of diverse European powers under a singular cause displayed a rare moment of unity in an era often marked by internecine conflicts. The strategic deployment of naval tactics, the precise coordination amongst fleets, and the sheer audacity of facing a formidable adversary reinforce the importance of calculated risk and collective resolve.

The immediate aftermath of the Battle of Lepanto signaled a gradual decline in Ottoman naval dominance and instilled a renewed vigor in Christian Europe. Furthermore, it catalyzed significant changes in naval warfare, prompting advancements that would redefine military engagements in subsequent centuries. The psychological impact on both the victors and the defeated emphasized the enduring power of morale and belief.

Across the artistic and literary landscapes, the Battle of Lepanto found enduring expressions. Contemporary accounts and later depictions immortalized the clash, weaving it into the cultural memory of Europe. These artistic renditions served not only as historical records but as inspirational narratives that extolled the virtues of bravery, faith, and divine intervention. They ensured that the legacy of Lepanto would persist through generations, influencing even modern interpretations of heroism and spirituality.

In a broader historical perspective, the Battle of Lepanto transcends its immediate temporal confines, offering lessons for modern times. It serves as a poignant reminder of the strength found in unity and faith, principles that are just as relevant today. The reevaluation of this battle and its broader historical contexts reveals the complexity of historical causation and the enduring influence of seemingly singular events.

Ultimately, the intertwined stories of the Holy House of Loreto, the Holy Rosary, and the Battle of Lepanto underscore a narrative of divine orchestration and human agency. They illustrate how history is not merely a series of random events but a coherent story woven with purpose and meaning. For Roman Catholics, strategists, and historians alike, these themes offer rich insights into the nature of faith, the dynamics of power, and the timeless struggle between opposing forces in shaping our world. The legacy of these events continues to inspire and challenge us, urging reflection on the forces that underpin our history and the values that sustain our societies.

Appendix A: Appendix

Maps and Diagrams

This section includes a collection of maps and diagrams to help visualize the events and locations discussed throughout the book. The maps provide detailed geographical contexts, illustrating the strategic movements and placements of the Christian and Ottoman fleets during the Battle of Lepanto. Additionally, diagrams present the architectural layout and historical sites of the Holy House of Loreto, accentuating its significance in both spiritual and historical contexts.

List of Major Participants

The following is a comprehensive list of the key figures who played crucial roles in the events surrounding the Battle of Lepanto. This includes leaders, commanders, and significant contributors from both the Christian and Ottoman sides. The list is intended to offer readers a quick reference point for understanding the broader narrative and identifying the individuals who shaped this pivotal moment in history.

- Don Juan of Austria
- Ali Pasha
- Saint Pius V

- Marcantonio Colonna
- Andrea Doria
- Uluc Ali
- Sebastiano Venier
- Additional commanders and warriors

Prayers and Devotions Related to the Battle and the Holy House of Loreto

This section compiles significant prayers and devotions that have been historically associated with the Battle of Lepanto and the Holy House of Loreto. These prayers not only reflect the spirituality of the time but also emphasize the unwavering faith that influenced the course of events. They provide a deeper understanding of the religious fervor and devotion that underpinned the Christian forces' resolve.

1. **Prayer of Thanksgiving after the Battle**

   "Almighty and ever-living God, we give thanks for Your providence in guiding and protecting us during the great Battle of Lepanto. As we commemorate our victory, we remember the courage of the men who fought and the unity of the Christian nations. Grant us the strength to continue in faith and the wisdom to seek peace."

2. **The Litany of the Holy House of Loreto**

"Lord, have mercy on us.

Christ, have mercy on us.

Lord, have mercy on us. Christ, hear us.

Christ, graciously hear us.

God the Father of Heaven, have mercy on us.

God the Son, Redeemer of the world, have mercy on us.

God the Holy Spirit, have mercy on us.

Holy Trinity, one God, have mercy on us.

Our Lady of Loreto, pray for us.

Holy Mary, pray for us.
Queen of the Holy Rosary, pray for us.
Queen of Victories, pray for us.
..."

These included prayers are but a small representation of the extensive devotions associated with the Holy House of Loreto and the historical triumphs celebrated by the Catholic faith. They serve as a testament to the enduring legacy of faith that has transcended centuries, inspiring countless generations in their spiritual journeys.

Maps and Diagrams

In illuminating the historical complexities and honorable triumphs associated with the Holy House of Loreto, the Holy Rosary, and the pivotal Battle of Lepanto, maps and diagrams serve as invaluable tools. These visual aids not only enhance comprehension but also foster a deeper appreciation for the geospatial and strategic elements embedded in these narratives. The following section elucidates the function and importance of various maps and diagrams in contextualizing these interwoven historical events.

Maps constitute a foundational aspect of understanding the cultural and strategic milieu in which these events transpired. Consider, for instance, a map delineating the territorial expanse of the Ottoman Empire during the 16th century. Such a map illustrates the enormity of the Islamic power that the Christian European forces were up against, highlighting regions of strategic importance. This backdrop is essential for appreciating the subsequent military maneuvers and battles.

Similarly, a detailed map of the Mediterranean Sea, particularly focusing on the Gulf of Patras where the Battle of Lepanto took place, serves to underscore the nautical challenges and strategic considerations that influenced naval engagements. This map shows the navigable routes and key positions, imparting a sense of the geographical constraints and opportunities available to both the Holy League and Ottoman fleets.

In the context of the Holy House of Loreto, maps tracing its purported journey from Nazareth to Loreto are of exceptional interest. These maps give visual substance to the legend of its miraculous transportation by angels, stopping by several European locations before reaching its final resting place in Loreto, Italy. The visual representation of this miraculous journey amplifies the narrative's mystique, allowing the viewers to trace the route and the lore surrounding it. Such maps not only capture the imagination but also entwine the sacred with the geographic.

Diagrams also hold considerable importance, particularly in the explanation of naval tactics and formations used in the Battle of Lepanto. Detailed diagrams depicting the deployment of the Holy League's galleys versus the Ottoman fleet offer insights into the strategic ingenuity that characterized this epic confrontation. These diagrams can illustrate the famed echelon formation used by the Christian forces, allowing for a better grasp of tactical decisions that led to their victory.

Furthermore, a schematic representation of the Holy House of Loreto itself provides a tangible connection to a revered object of faith. Such diagrams may include architectural details and spatial arrangements that are critical for understanding both its spiritual and cultural significance. They might also compare the Holy House with typical first-century Judean homes, situating the relic within its historical and cultural context.

Maps and diagrams related to Saint Pius V's mobilization of the Christian alliance are also of profound significance. A map showing the principal cities and regions where influential figures converged to form the Holy League brings into focus the geopolitical landscape of the time. Diagrams outlining the chain of command and the distribution of responsibilities among the allied forces offer an organized view of how unity was achieved in diversity—a testament to the strategic acumen and diplomatic prowess of Saint Pius V.

A map detailing the journey of the Christian fleet from Messina to the Gulf of Patras reveals the logistical challenges faced by the Holy League. It showcases the various ports visited, the perils of the open sea, and the tactical stops made to gather intelligence and supply provisions. Such a map underscores the arduous endeavor of coordinating disparate fleets into a single formidable force.

One cannot overlook the importance of diagrams that portray the sequence of events during the Battle of Lepanto itself. A timeline overlaid with pivotal moments can serve as a multi-dimensional diagram, featuring not only temporal but also spatial information. This can indicate the initial alignments, the first engagements, crucial turning points, and the final clash, providing a comprehensive overview of the battle's dynamics.

For a more intimate understanding of personal contributions, diagrams that depict the positioning and movements of key personalities on both sides are invaluable. For instance, the positions of Don Juan of Austria and Ali Pasha during critical moments of the battle can be juxtaposed to reflect their leadership styles and strategic decisions. Such diagrams humanize the battle, transforming it from an abstract clash of forces to a vivid narrative of human endeavor and valor.

Moreover, maps showing the post-battle reconstruction and redistribution of territories help contextualize the immediate aftermath of the Battle of Lepanto. These maps can highlight geopolitical shifts and the realignment of power structures within the Mediterranean basin, emphasizing the battle's long-lasting impact.

It is also worthwhile to include diagrams that depict the influence of the battle on subsequent naval warfare. For example, illustrations comparing ship designs and armaments before and after the battle provide insights into technological and tactical evolutions prompted by this landmark encounter. Such diagrams serve as silent witnesses to the enduring legacy of the Battle of Lepanto on maritime history.

Maps illustrating the spread and influence of the Holy Rosary after the battle reflect its significance as a devotional practice. From Europe to the farthest reaches of the New World, the proliferation of the Rosary underscores its role in shaping spiritual lives and communities. A map tracing such influences provides a visual testament to the Rosary's enduring appeal and spiritual potency.

Lastly, a composite map integrating various layers of information —territorial bounds, naval routes, pilgrimage paths, and post-battle realignments—serves as a masterful tool for an overarching view. This comprehensive map encapsulates the intertwined narratives of faith, strategy, and providence that define the essence of this book.

In conclusion, maps and diagrams transcend mere illustrative purposes. They are indispensable instruments that distill complex narratives into accessible visual forms, enriching our understanding of the Holy House of Loreto, the Holy Rosary, and the Battle of Lepanto. By offering a tangible link to the past, they invite us to explore these monumental events with heightened clarity and reverence.

List of Major Participants

The participants in the Battle of Lepanto were a mixture of influential figures, ranging from monarchs to military commanders, whose contributions cemented the alliance and shaped the outcome of this historical clash. Each individual brought unique capabilities and harboring distinct motivations, yet their collective efforts fostered a coordinated resistance against the formidable Ottoman Empire.

Don Juan of Austria, who was the illegitimate son of Holy Roman Emperor Charles V and half-brother to King Philip II of Spain, emerged as the leading figure of the Holy League's naval forces. Don Juan's experience, valor, and exceptional command capabilities played a critical role in orchestrating the Christian fleet's strategy and tactics. His charismatic leadership and resolve were indispensable, and they brought together a coalition of diverse nations under a unified purpose.

On the opposite side stood Ali Pasha, the high-ranking Ottoman naval commander entrusted by Sultan Selim II to lead the empire's fleet. Ali Pasha, known for his strategic acumen and fierce determination, was tasked with expanding the Ottoman's maritime dominance. His command decisions and defense strategies were pivotal, creating a formidable challenge for the Holy League's forces.

Among the ranks of the Holy League, several notables such as Marcantonio Colonna and Sebastiano Venier contributed significantly. Colonna, a seasoned naval commander from a noble Italian family, served as the commander of the papal fleet. His expertise and bravery in naval warfare proved invaluable during the intense phases of the battle. Similarly, Venier, who was the Doge of Venice, brought with him a wealth of maritime experience and a fierce loyalty to the Venetian Republic. Both commanders played crucial roles in coordinating attacks and rallying their fleets amidst the chaotic engagements.

From the Spanish contingent, Gianandrea Doria, a Genoese admiral, was known for his keen strategic mind and command over the left-wing of the Christian fleet. Doria's ability to maneuver his ships with precision and execute complex battle plans significantly contributed to the disruption of the Ottoman formation.

Another key figure was Agostino Barbarigo, the Venetian commander who led the right wing of the Holy League's fleet. Barbarigo's leadership was characterized by boldness and tactical innovation, which were instrumental in outflanking the advanced Ottoman squadrons. His bravery, however, came at a great cost, as he sustained mortal wounds during the intense confrontations.

On the Ottoman side, key figures such as Lala Kara Mustafa Pasha, who was the Grand Vizier and instrumental in the empire's Mediterranean campaigns, and Uluç Ali Reis, commander of the left-wing of the Ottoman fleet, were pivotal. Uluç Ali's expertise in naval warfare was demonstrated through his adeptness in commanding several successful engagements prior to, and during, the Battle of Lepanto. The resilience and tactical finesse displayed by these commanders made them formidable adversaries.

King Philip II of Spain also played a significant indirect role. While not physically present at the battle, his political and financial support were essential in assembling the Holy League. His steadfast Christians, combined with his resources, facilitated the procurement of vital ships, arms, and men.

Pope Pius V, who was instrumental in forming the Holy League, cannot be overlooked. Through his diplomatic channels and spiritual encouragement, he unified the Christian forces under a single banner to face the looming Ottoman threat. His devotion and unyielding intercessions were seen as spiritually bolstering the morale of the fleet. His institution of the Holy Rosary among the warriors provided them with a unifying spiritual practice and readied them for the impending battle.

Each participant's contribution, whether direct or indirect, wove together a tale of collective valor, strategy, and sacrifice. The amalgamation of naval prowess, relentless leadership, and unwavering faith determined the course of the battle. The aforementioned individuals epitomized the decisive roles and monumental efforts of the on-ground commanders and the political figures who orchestrated the monumental clash that shaped the course of history on that fateful day in October 1571.

Understanding the various contributions of these significant figures not only allows us to appreciate the complexities involved in the Battle of Lepanto but also illuminates the broader narrative. The synthesis of their capabilities, decisions, and sacrifices created a turning point that resonated far beyond their lifetimes, impacting religious, political, and military trajectories in Europe for centuries to come.

Prayers and Devotions Related to the Battle and the Holy House of Loreto

The Battle of Lepanto holds an unparalleled place in both military history and the spiritual narrative of Christianity. For many Roman Catholics, its significance is magnified through the lens of divine intervention and the powerful intercession of the Holy Virgin, specifically through the Holy Rosary. Devotional practices that emerged during and after this momentous event emphasize not only the power of prayer but also the connection to the Holy House of Loreto, believed by many to be the house where the Virgin Mary lived.

The origins of the prayers dedicated to Our Lady of Victory can be traced back to the fervent devotion that Pope Pius V encouraged among Christian faithful. Central to these prayers was the Holy Rosary. On the eve of the battle, a multitude of supplications and invocations were raised to the heavens, with the Holy Rosary being the focal point. Pope Pius V called upon the entire Christian world to participate in a rosary crusade to implore the Blessed Virgin for a miraculous intervention.

Following the triumph at Lepanto, prayers of thanksgiving proliferated. One of the most notable was the prayer of thanks offered by Pope Pius V himself. He attributed the victory to the intercession of the Virgin Mary and the unified prayers of the Christian faithful. Never before had the power of collective prayer been so visibly demonstrated, creating a profound sense of spiritual solidarity among European Christians.

It is impossible to separate the Holy House of Loreto from this narrative. Devotion to the Holy House predates the battle, rooted in the belief that angels transported Mary's house from Nazareth to Loreto. This belief added an extra layer of spiritual significance to the devotions surrounding the battle. The Holy House became a pilgrimage destination for those seeking to offer prayers of gratitude for the miraculous victory. Historical records show an increase in pilgrimages following the battle, as pilgrims came to honor the Virgin Mary in the very place connected to her earthly life.

The Litany of Loreto, also known as the Litany of the Blessed Virgin Mary, became an essential part of Marian devotions tied to the battle. Its use was encouraged to invoke Mary's intercession not just for protection in times of war, but also for personal supplications and community needs. The litany's origins lie in the Marian shrine at Loreto, but its widespread usage during and after the Battle of Lepanto underscores its importance.

The prayers and devotions that emerged out of this historical backdrop were not confined to the immediate aftermath of the battle. They have been perpetuated through generations, demonstrating their enduring power. The Feast of Our Lady of Victory, later renamed the

Feast of Our Lady of the Rosary, was established to commemorate the victory and to continuously remind the faithful of the power of prayer and divine intercession. Celebrated on October 7th, this feast day is marked by special rosary prayers, Masses, and processions.

Part of the devotion that connects the Battle of Lepanto and the Holy House of Loreto is the emphasis on community prayer. The solidarity displayed during the rosary crusade called by Pope Pius V laid a foundation for how communal prayer could achieve what individual efforts could not. This collective action has remained a hallmark of Catholic practice, particularly in times of trials and tribulations.

It's noteworthy that many of the devotional practices that developed have remained relevant. The recitation of the Rosary remains a vital aspect of Catholic life. It serves as both a form of personal meditation and a communal prayer. The events of the Battle of Lepanto serve as a historical testimony to the effectiveness of these spiritual exercises, encouraging continued devotion among the faithful.

The intertwining of the Holy House of Loreto with the Battle of Lepanto is further enriched by various accounts of miracles attributed to Mary's intercession. These accounts, though numerous and varied, collectively attest to the unwavering faith placed in the Virgin Mary. They serve as powerful stories passed down through centuries, reaffirming the belief in the miraculous.

Ultimately, the prayers and devotions stemming from the Battle of Lepanto and the Holy House of Loreto carve out a unique space in the annals of Christian spirituality. They represent a blend of historical reality and divine mystery, a testament to the belief that earthly affairs can indeed be influenced by heavenly intervention. This duality serves as a cornerstone for Roman Catholics, reinforcing their spiritual practices and their historical consciousness.

As modern devotees continue to engage in these prayers and devotions, they perpetuate a rich tradition that began centuries ago. They connect to a legacy of faith that transcends generations, reminding them that the powerful intercession of the Virgin Mary and the unifying force of collective prayer are as relevant today as they were on that fateful day in 1571.

www.ingramcontent.com/pod-product-compliance
Lightning Source LLC
Chambersburg PA
CBHW072008150726
47999CB00002B/554